VICTORS
AND
VICTIMS

ARE YOU BEING HELD BACK BY A VICTIM MENTALITY?

K . R . H A R R I S O N

Authentic

Victors and Victims
Copyright © 2014
K.R. Harrison

Cover design by Rob Williams, InsideOut Design
Edited by Keith Wall

Published by Authentic Publishers
188 Front Street, Suite 116-44
Franklin, TN 37064

Authentic Publishers is a division of
Authentic Media, Inc.

Library of Congress Cataloging-in-Publication Data

Harrison, K.R.
Victors and Victims : Are you being held back by a victim mentality? / K.R. Harrison

p. cm.
ISBN 978-1-78078-126-6
978-1-78078-254-6 (e-book)

Printed in the United States of America

21 20 19 18 17 16 15 14   10 9 8 7 6 5 4 3 2 1

Contents

Introduction 5

PART ONE:
The Problem with Victims, the Power of Victors

1. Say You Want a Revolution . . . in Taking Responsibility........ 11
2. The Choice Is Yours... 23
3. Managing Choice.. 33
4. Ambition: The Art of Aiming High 47
5. The Language of Leadership 55
6. Victims in Life 63
7. Victors in Life... 73

PART TWO:
Striving for Solutions: Empowering Victor
Attitudes and Actions

8. Making "Market Force" Work for You 83
9. The Four Styles in Action 111
10. A Closer Look at Styles.. 133
11. Hidden Thoughts and Inner Hauntings.................... 149
12. Waiting Your Turn.. 159
13. Interdependent Communities................................ 167
14. Common Questions and Misunderstandings.............. 175

Final Thoughts 187

Introduction

My assistant told me John Cundiff was on the phone. Odd. John was a well-known business coach who taught billionaires, CEOs of international companies, and famous college basketball coaches. He was also known for being an extremely demanding teacher and for firing clients who didn't seem to "get it." John Cundiff didn't just call a stranger for a friendly chat.

About a year earlier, I had participated in a six-week course taught by John in which several executives met on a weekly conference call. I heard him yell at company presidents and insult those who were less than totally committed. On the first call, one of the participants joined late. John berated him for not being committed enough and ordered him off the phone and out of his course. To take a course from John Cundiff, one had better bring the best game they had and be ready to drink from a fire hose of wisdom.

One didn't just pick up the phone and call John, so to have him waiting on the line to talk to me was intriguing.

I picked up the phone. "This is Ken," I said.

"Do you have what it takes to be a ruthless leader?"

That was all he said, in an intense, matter-of-fact voice.

"Well . . ."

"To be ruthless is to be without mercy for your own faults and the faults of others. Will you be ruthless in your commitment to your intention to build your company into the organization that reflects your values?"

How do you answer that? I was the CEO of a national company with offices in twenty-eight cities. Frankly, I was used to people kissing up to me, not calling unannounced and demanding direct answers to tough questions. I hesitated. To answer yes would be a serious commitment to whatever his offer was, but to answer no was to lose whatever opportunity was about to be presented.

John kept talking. "We are in a time of failing organizations and failing leaders. You are one of the few true leaders I have come across. Are you willing to accept your destiny as a true leader? Can you be ruthless?"

I barely knew John. I had taken his conference call course reluctantly. As a graduate of Marine Corps Officer Candidate School, a veteran of the Los Angeles Police Department, and a successful businessman and CEO for several years, I couldn't see why I needed a business "coach." When someone pointed out that even Tom Brady has a quarterback coach and Tiger Woods has a golf coach, I agreed maybe it was worth hearing out a business coach. After one call with John, I was painfully aware of how little I knew.

Now I thought for a moment and swallowed hard. "Yes," I said.

"Then we will have a one-hour call once a week. Have your assistant call mine to set up the times." He hung up.

That call came in late 2008. The bond markets had crashed a few months earlier and with it my company's entire market. Firms were slashing costs and laying off people in record numbers to try to survive what would become the biggest commercial real estate recession in history. Our company had amassed considerable debt in an effort to save employees, and we had several offices and departments mired in mediocrity. It seemed that no matter what I did, the mediocre performance stayed that way. No reward system, threats, or motivational speeches could change the complacency of people who saw layoffs happening all over the industry.

Then I started to listen to John. While our two biggest competitors cut their staff in half over the next two years, we doubled revenues and increased profit by 300 percent from our previous high marks. The complacent employees left in droves, replaced by motivated, eager people. While our competitors were firing, we were hiring.

That wasn't all. The same principles I applied at work made me a better husband, father, and friend. My closest relationships were strengthened and deepened. What's more, I learned to recognize and eliminate the unhealthy relationships in my life that simply drained time and energy.

The world needs a large dose of what John is teaching. Many of the ideas I present in this book I learned from John, fortified with my own real-world experience and lessons. This is wisdom that applies to all of life—business, marriage, parenting, friendships, service projects, and spiritual pursuits. These are the simple yet powerful ideas that have existed for thousands of years but the western world has lost its grasp of them. Its time to come back to what we already know is true.

Victors and Victims unveils the truth that people who find success and joy in life are those who know who they are and *give* of themselves . . . versus those who know what they want and *take* for themselves.

Success in life comes in many different forms. Profitable careers and businesses come to mind, but what about happy marriages, well-raised kids, loyal friendships? Success, no matter what its form, has the same foundations. Mastering them means mastering life.

We all have different core passions. Some yearn for freedom, some for security; some dwell on the past and some on the future. Our core passions dictate how we communicate and what messages and beliefs we listen to and follow. When you understand your own core passions as well as those of the people around you, you can communicate successfully and form powerful relationships filled with joy and promise.

In the pages ahead, I draw from my experiences fighting violent crime as a police officer in Los Angeles, leading international companies, and my long-term marriage and decades of raising children in order to give you the keys to turning ambition into success.

By sharing these ideas and insights, I want to help you . . .

- Understand how to identify whether you have a Victim mentality or a Victor mentality—whether you are part of the problem in relationships or part of the solution.
- Form an identity and offer something redeeming to the people in your life, so you can be a solution to others' problems.
- Listen and speak in ways that cause others to hear and receive what you say.
- Understand your own and others' inherent weaknesses so you can improve your life and empathize with others.
- Recognize your own and others strengths so you can form productive teams that maximize the effectiveness of the group.

Without a doubt, you want to be a victor and not a victim . . . and you want the same for your spouse, children, friends, coworkers, staff members, and fellow church members. I'm confident that if you absorb and apply the principles I share, you will greatly enrich your own life and the lives of those around you.

PART ONE

THE PROBLEM WITH VICTIMS, THE POWER OF VICTORS

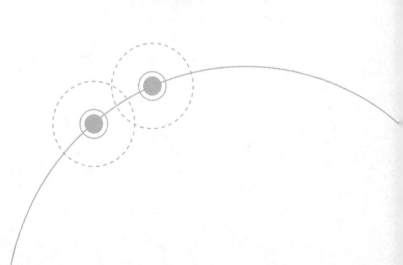

1

SAY YOU WANT A REVOLUTION...
IN TAKING RESPONSIBILITY

America was not built on fear. America was built
on courage, on imagination, and an unbeatable
determination to do the job at hand.

Harry S. Truman

I loved being a Los Angeles police officer . . . and I hated it. I was assigned to South-Central Los Angeles, which most people know as Watts. Gun battles, car pursuits, and chasing armed suspects through streets and alleys were normal parts of the day. Those were the things I loved. Few things are as rewarding as arresting criminals and seeing the relief and gratitude on the faces of their victims.

What I hated was the constant second-guessing of everything we did. My fellow officers and I were dropped into mass chaos where we made life-and-death decisions at great risk to others and ourselves. Often those situations involved violence, with decisions made while adrenaline pumped through our veins.

Later, we wrote detailed reports about all of it—every word spoken, every thought we had, every action taken. Analysts read those reports and told us what we did wrong. I felt as if I was always in trouble, always feeling like I was being called to the principal's office.

I couldn't wait to get back on the streets risking my life again, leaving the analysts to their criticism. To me, the streets weren't danger; they were freedom.

The defining moment came on a hot afternoon. My partner and I had just chased down a gang member with the 83rd Street Crips, known as the Eight-Trey Crips. We had wrestled a gun from him and had him in the back of our car as we drove to the 77th Division jail. Though we were still out of breath and battered from his arrest, we took a detour down 56th Street, a major drug-dealing block where there had been a rash of recent murders.

As we turned a corner, we saw a man in a car parked on the side of the road screaming at us and waving his hands. Blood was erupting from his head and draining down his face. Behind him I saw a man's head sticking up from the back seat, a gun shoved into the driver's neck.

"Gun!" I yelled and jammed the car to the curb.

The man from the back seat jumped out of the car, still holding the gun. Just as I got out of the car, he turned to shoot, but I jumped to my left so he had to turn around in the other direction to aim at me. Just as he turned and raised his gun, I drew and fired. His body collapsed like someone had just yanked the skeleton from it.

I ran to him and kicked the gun from his hand. His eyes stared lifelessly at the glaring sun.

Thus began one of the brutal and stressful lessons of my life. The shooting wasn't stressful. It was less than ten seconds from the time we saw the driver to the time a man lay dead at my feet. There was no time to think, only react. The stressful part was when the analysts descended to dissect and examine every action taken, every step made. In less than a minute, the block was filled with police cars. A sergeant pulled me away from my partner and whisked me back to the station. In the car mirror, I could see another sergeant grabbing my partner.

At the station, my partner, John, and I were told we couldn't speak to each other, and we were watched by the two sergeants. John was one of my best friends. We carpooled to work together, our wives shopped together. Less than ten minutes after such violence, sergeants were babysitting us.

Soon four homicide detectives appeared. Two interviewed me while two interviewed John. The questions went on for hours. The detectives tried to act friendly, but their questions were laced with suspicion and skepticism.

"Officer Harrison, you hungry? You want some pizza?"

I didn't want pizza.

"I'll order you some pizza." The pizza came and the detectives ate it.

Four hours later, John and I were brought back to the scene. We were ordered not to speak to each other as we spent several hours walking the detectives through an event that took ten seconds. Drug dealers gathered around to commentate on our walk-through: "Yep, that's what happened! They shot him right there. Good thing, too—he was mean! Glad those cops shot him!"

The detectives tried to shoo the dealers away, but they were enjoying the show. I was placed on paid leave for three days until my superiors could get me in to see a department psychologist, who interviewed me for less than five minutes before stamping a piece of paper proclaiming me fit for duty.

The investigation revealed that the man I'd shot was a notorious killer, and we had interrupted a planned drug hit. The man had pretended to be a drug buyer to get into the victim's car with the intent to execute him. Then we turned down that street, still trying to catch our breath from the gang member we were on our way to booking.

All of a sudden, the investigation was over. That was it. Just as the storm clouds of suspicion and doubt had instantaneously appeared above my head, they blew away just as quickly.

I went from being the focus of suspicion to being nominated for a medal. I felt angry and confused. No one showed up to congratulate me. No one apologized for treating me like a criminal. No one felt the need to; I had done my job as a street cop in the Los Angeles ghetto. They did their jobs as analysts. My job was to make a snap decision and risk my life to save others. Theirs was to analyze everything I did in detail, ensure it was within policy, and point out any mistakes I made so I could become a better officer and we could become a better police department.

I was aware of a strange thought, even back then. Those analysts liked what they did. They considered their duties important. They thought analyzing officer conduct on the streets and instructing them how to do it better had value.

I was vaguely aware of something else: not all the other officers were like me. I volunteered for the most dangerous assignments, took the worst calls, and was often the first one through the door when there was an armed suspect inside. Officers like us were affectionately named "gunfighters." But other officers preferred traffic duty, where they handled auto accidents and chased drunk drivers. Other officers wanted to be on surveillance duty, following suspects for weeks.

I noticed that we tended to divide up into cliques based on the type of law enforcement we preferred. The individuals in each group were very much alike. The personalities differed greatly, but there was something that linked all the gunfighters, analysts, traffic cops, and detectives within their respective groups. Rivalries developed among the various groups, and the gunfighters were pretty sure we were the real LAPD and everyone else were just pretenders.

There was no interdependence between the factions; there was independence. We all wanted to save the world, and we were sure ours was the only way to do it. Rather than being good at what we did and respecting the others to be good at what they did, we resented each other.

I had the impression that a true LA police officer's job was to chase down bad guys, book them, and forget about them. Something might happen later—I could be subpoenaed to testify against the bad guys—but that was all. Nothing else was really important, and I certainly wasn't responsible for whatever transpired.

Fast-forward twenty years: Along with ten partners, I sold a company to a $4 billion conglomerate, and I had become the CEO. I was running it the same way I policed the streets of Los Angeles. If I could communicate the vision to people with passion, hold the executives accountable, negotiate the right contracts, appease the board and give great speeches, we'd be successful.

Other people in the company did stuff . . . but nothing else was really important, was it? I had brought the same "disease" of mind and spirit with me through all the success. The disease was that it was all about me—my way, my style, my plan.

When John Cundiff called to ask if I could be a "ruthless leader," I was exhausted. I had been running a company filled with people who had the same attitude I did. They had little concern for how they fit in to the overall company, what value they brought, or what anyone else did. They were sure of one thing: they were valuable, even though most didn't really know what their contribution to the company was.

I was, as the cliché goes, herding cats and running out of energy. So what changed? What was John Cundiff's offer and why was it so effective? The fact is that we have lost the idea that each individual listens differently, thinks differently, and brings different intentions to an organization. Someone may see a blunt person as refreshingly to the point, another may see him as offensive and harsh. This is because people are listening for different things in a conversation.

Often it isn't that people can't hear; it is that they can't hear *you*. We tend to talk to people in the way that we listen, instead of how *they* listen. John Cundiff's principles taught me to understand the ways in which people think and hear so I could encourage them in their inherent intentions and skills. I learned to *pull* people instead of *push* them. I learned to create a vacuum of opportunity that people rushed to fill, rather than to dominate them with flowery speeches and grandiose goals.

What's Old Is New

This teaching is as ancient as the Bible, where the apostle Paul talks about the people of the church all bringing different skills to the "body," and how they were all equally valuable (1 Corinthians 12:12-26). John's coaching not only helped to turn a mediocre company into a national powerhouse in the middle of a recession, it also helped me in many aspects of my life. Once I learned to understand how my wife, kids, and friends listened, I also learned to communicate in ways they could hear and understand. Once I understood my own nuances, I was able to see where natural breakdowns occurred in my own listening.

As a society, we lost our way long ago, but the breakdown is only now showing up in major ways. Since World War II, America has been dominated by strong command-and-control organizations (companies, churches, nonprofits, educational institutions, and so on). These were inherently broken, but as leaders forced people into teams, the people adapted in order to survive. Organizations with leaders who instinctively built the right teams grew, while those that did not failed.

We are now in a crisis because we no longer accept the assertions of our leaders. Not long ago, we gave respect to people based on their position of authority. Teachers, parents, police officers, bosses, politicians, clergy, or any other form of perceived authority received reverence based on the position they held. Now we have an opposite perspective of leaders, insisting they prove their trustworthiness to us before we will give them respect. In order for leaders to build effective organizations, they must learn to communicate in ways that people will hear.

Rebellion has always been at the heart of who we are as Americans. Our nation was founded through revolution. We rejected tyranny by discarding the opinion that some people had a right to rule, and turned to democracy where people had to earn the privilege to lead. We rejected European rule in order to pursue opportunity unhindered by stereotypes and class limitations.

The United States is a country that is unique to the world in its ability to create, produce, and sustain new ideas and consistent growth. It is the only country in history that became a power by production and innovation rather than by conquering and looting.

This is quite simply because we have been a nation of Victors. Those who originally populated the continent from Europe were brave pioneers who risked everything for a chance to make their own opportunities. It has been a nation of interdependent people cooperating to build something amazing. America was built by strong, self-sufficient, creative immigrants who traded stability for opportunity and freedom. One could say this is the essence of the American Spirit.

The U.S. has been a land where people have equality of opportunity. No matter the class, race, nationality, or any other distinction of its people, the U.S. has continued a constant arc of growth and increasing freedom since its inception, whereas a constant stream of oppressive nations have risen and collapsed. This is because the U.S. foundation of equality of opportunity sustains itself by attracting those with ambition and skill. The socialist foundation of equality of outcome necessarily depends on the most talented people to carry the burden of society while receiving no incentive to do so.

We are now at a crossroads. The Victors have succeeded in creating a wonderful country, filled with opportunity. This originally attracted those striving to partake in the success of the Victors, those demanding equality of opportunity, rather than Victims, who demand equality of outcome. According to Charles Bronson, who was a coalminer in West Virginia before he became an actor, "A man works his whole life to make enough money to give to his children, so they don't have to go through what made him a man in the first place."

One can see, in these troubled times, that the Victims in this country have seized control. Victims demand rights rather than opportunity. Hoards of our young people choose to protest on Wall Street rather than create opportunities for themselves. Rather than appeal to private industry with their skills, they appeal to the government for their rights.

We hear people constantly wax nostalgic about the "good ol' days" in America, but what were those? In the good ol' days, racism was accepted, children were abused because no one talked about it, and women couldn't vote. When people speak of the "good ol' America," they usually point to something like TVs shows such as *Father Knows Best* or *Leave it to Beaver*, which were portraits of something that never existed.

A man works his whole life to make enough money
to give to his children, so they don't have to go through
what made him a man in the first place.

Charles Bronson

But something *did* exist that they're referring to. What they are thinking of are the days when Victors outnumbered Victims . . . when Americans demanded hard work from themselves and those around them through strong, interdependent communities . . . when there was genuine respect for authority because authority figures were respectable . . . when entrepreneurs were celebrated and emulated.

Victors take a proactive approach to life. They don't believe they are confined to their current position, choosing instead to continuously seek ways to improve their situation. Victors just want to know what the opportunity is. They don't need to be convinced, cajoled, or coaxed in order to perform. They don't wait to hear the details on the dental plan or whether there is a matching 401(k). Victors hear the offer, process the opportunity, and yell, "Pick me!"

The unrest we feel in the changing morality around us is our observation that more and more people are Victims, who believe that life happens to them and there is nothing they can do to change it. They believe that someone else can and should improve their lot in life, and they demand that those around them make them happy. They spend their lives in fear about what will come next. Victims are just trying to survive in life and have their focus squarely on themselves.

When I first became a CEO, the biggest shock I had was how often people use a "code phrase" for fear in their discussions: "What if?" Such as . . .

"What if we fail?"

"What if they don't want to buy our product?"

"What if something better comes along?"

"What if there's an accident?"

What if really just means "I'm afraid." Years ago when my wife and I did marriage counseling, we heard similar code words: "What if my husband doesn't get a good job?" "What if my wife cheats on me?" "What if our kids won't listen to us?"

The reason Victims are afraid is because they believe they don't have a choice. "I was born this way!" "I'm an addict—it's a disease." "I came from a terrible family background—I can't change that." Thought patterns like these are what make Victims dangerous. Since they had no choice, they have no accountability for results. Since they believe they can't improve their situation, they become adept at assigning blame.

It is important to note that Victims never recognize this in themselves. Filled with stories about why "it" is not their fault and on dwelling on the failure of others to take care of them, these people have deep resentment of anyone who tries to hold them accountable to their own actions. Victors accept responsibility and constructive criticism because of an inherent desire to sharpen their skills to take advantage of opportunity. In fact, one of the easiest ways to differentiate Victims and Victors is their willingness to accept responsibility.

The Road Ahead

History is littered with the carcasses of once-great nations whose citizens traded freedom for security. Sometimes it's fast like the

Germans knowingly abdicating their freedom by electing the Nazis to power in exchange for promises of jobs and social justice. Sometimes it is slow, like the empire of Greece, whose citizens gave up their freedom for empty promises of security. That once-great nation now has an economy smaller than fourteen U.S. states.

The future of our nation does not depend on changing the Victims. They will not change. It depends on the reaction of the Victors. We can react in one of three ways: resignation, rage, or revolution.

A primary difference between Victors and Victims is that one group turns their anger inward and the other turns it outward. Revolutionaries understand that the only way to prosperity is to show other Victors a better way. They turn to revolution in the original American sense. They choose to throw off the tyranny of Victims and create opportunity.

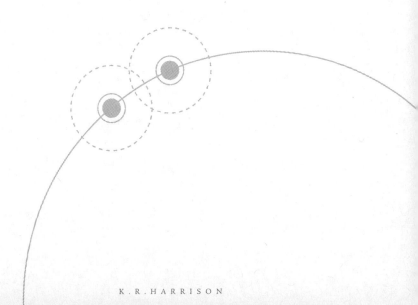

2

THE CHOICE IS YOURS

No action could be lower or more futile
than for one person to throw upon another than
the burden of his abdication of choice.

Ayn Rand

People who can acknowledge and make choices are successful. The CEO of a Fortune 500 company and the chronically unsuccessful person each has the same amount of time. The difference between the two is that the CEO makes many more choices—wise choices—in his time.

The unsuccessful person avoids choice and spends his time explaining to himself and anyone who will listen how he really has no choice. For every scenario, he has an explanation.

"I'm this way because my father . . . "

"I can't get a job because my back . . . "

"I drink too much because when I was a kid . . . "

The statement only matters up to "because." Everything after "because" is simply a story. What the person is saying is, "I'm this way," "I can't get a job," "I drink too much." The unsuccessful person simply represents the most foundational level of avoidance of choice. Employees, spouses, our children, our friends—they do it, too. They avoid choice and then have their story. "Her kids are so much better behaved than mine because . . . He starts for the lacrosse team in front of me because . . . If only this company did [fill in the blank], then I could succeed . . . If only my husband [fill in the blank], then I would be a better wife . . . As soon as [fill in the blank], I'll start playing catch with my son."

The managing director (MD) of one of our offices called me to complain that she couldn't be successful because . . . When she was finished with her story, I pointed out that her regional branch was the same in size, personnel, and market penetration as four other offices: Denver, Honolulu, Phoenix, and Columbus. The MDs of those offices all ranked as some of the top earners in our firm. I asked her to explain why they were all successful despite having the same set of circumstances she did. She had no answer, because she had spent her time prepping her story instead of researching changes that would lead to success.

The Acceleration of Choice

Because life is about transactions and transactions involve choice, successful people make choices quicker and force choice more often. When it comes to making choices faster, education, experience, mental capacity, and other factors have their place. But the most important accelerator of choice in our lifetimes has been technology. Think of the ability to make a choice in negotiations with Europe 200 years ago. A letter was written and put on a ship, which sailed across the sea, and then a letter of response was sent back—across the sea. It wasn't always certain both letters were received, and the process could take six months.

The telegraph allowed for limited information transfer . . . then the telephone . . . then the telex . . . then the fax machine . . . then email and texting and video conferencing. We can communicate with people on other continents without ever leaving our office chairs. Communicating with Europe is now easier than walking next door to talk to your neighbor. The acceleration of choice is unprecedented.

Modern relationships demand instant gratification. The pace of life has moved beyond our biological ability to keep up. The last 200 years have been a time of incredible advancements in technology.

It isn't the big that eat the small, it's the fast that eat the slow.

John Cundiff

Technological advancement is measured by what has been eliminated. Even our names indicate this. Automobiles were originally called "horseless carriages." We have wireless phones, cashless transactions, and unmanned spacecraft. Ultimately what we're measuring technology by is the elimination of steps in a process in order to speed up choice.

People too often stagnate, waiting for others to "come around." Instead, successful people force choice and move on. In the Marine Corps, we were taught that when you come to a fork in the road, take one and go with maximum effort. If you find it's the wrong road, turn around—but never hesitate at the fork. The motto that was drilled into our heads was, "The Marine who hesitates dies."

The ability to generate choice dictates success. Picture a mother with a lost child. She generates choice at incredible speed. She mobilizes the people around her to find the child. She doesn't stop to consider whether she's dressed appropriately or if her hair is neatly coiffed. She demands that people around her contribute with everything they have. She doesn't explain herself or tolerate people's stories about why they will or will not help. They must share in her focused intention with immediate and deliberate contribution or she will disregard them.

Victors are able to generate this kind of choice because they have the same passion and dedication as that mother does for her lost child. They demand immediate and total dedication to their intention and, though they articulate their vision for the future, they don't stop to explain themselves to critics. Victors don't have time for someone's story about why they can't contribute. They demand a choice.

Victors produce choices and don't live in regret over what might have been or what happened yesterday. There is always another transaction and the more time we live in regret over what could have been, the more we lose the ability to make choices in the present. Victims obsess on past failures and hurts, feeding a growing cancer of bitterness. As bitterness grows, the obsession with the past dominates and the ability to make choices in the present fades, Victims lose the potential to generate success. Their unconscious goal becomes recruiting other Victims to fill their daily need to review the past and ignore the present.

A Disaster Called "Mother's Day"

One of the worst days to work on the Los Angeles Police Department was what was dubbed "Mother's Day." This was not the annual holiday to honor mothers—it was the day welfare checks came out. It was called Mother's Day because of the enormous amount of drunken spousal abuse calls we got on those days. They were always emotionally draining, as our queue would fill with call after call of drunken men beating their wives, children, or girlfriends. Every one of those calls was dangerous and saddening as we dealt with enraged, inebriated people.

On one Mother's Day call, the wife screamed at my partner and I that her husband had been beating her. He loudly proclaimed his innocence—he hadn't done anything. Under California law, we were required to place him under arrest if the woman showed any signs of abuse, or if she wanted to press charges. When we started to arrest him, she decided she didn't want to press charges. Since she showed no physical signs of abuse, we had no choice but to release him. He was drunk and still very angry.

As usual, we separated her from her husband and beseeched her to get away to somewhere safe. She didn't want him arrested because that would just enrage him more, and he would be out of jail and back home within a few hours. She kept insisting that she couldn't leave, because she had nowhere else to go. We gave her the usual literature on women's shelters and other resources, but she insisted she didn't have a choice.

We took the man outside and told him to take a walk and not come back until he calmed down. We circled the block a few times to make sure he was walking away and then went on to the next abuse call, which would look just like this one. About an hour later, we were called back to the same location, which was also typical. When we arrived this time, however, the woman was dead and the man sat next to her with a gun on the table in front of him. As we arrested him, he explained that he didn't have a choice when he shot her—she had burned his dinner for the last time.

A domestic dispute turned into a 187 (murder) investigation because no one had a choice. She couldn't leave, despite the numerous options provided by the city of Los Angeles. He had to kill her because she couldn't get his dinner right. He didn't have a choice.

This story really isn't unusual. There isn't a big-city police officer in the U.S. who doesn't have many stories just like it. The absurdity of it, though, illustrates the nature of Victims. Though this is an extreme illustration, it shows the behavior of Victims at a fundamental level.

Educated people do and say similar things—they're simply more sophisticated about it. Encourage someone to visit their elderly grandmother and you'll hear, "Don't you think I want to? But I just don't have time! Do you know how much I work? My kids have to get to soccer practice! I'm on the PTA! If I had your life, maybe I could, but you just have no idea!"

> Each day in the school of life a lesson is taught.
> That lesson is repeated until learned.
>
> John Cundiff

Translation: I'm a good person and would do all those things, but I don't have a choice. You're a bad person for asking me, because your life is perfect and I'm a Victim. Answer them by asking about priorities, how they found five hours to play golf or six hours to watch two football games, when they could have taken just two hours to visit their grandmother. After that, just listen to their stories of victimhood: "I need golf to unwind. What's wrong with watching football?"

Victims avoid choice, even to their own detriment. Many times a new leader will be hated when he or she enacts change, even if it's for the good. That's because there will always be a segment of people who see any change as bad, no matter how much it improves a situation.

Victors clear the space for people to make choices. However, they must be steadfast in their resistance to having a vested interest in those choices. One of the hardest things for a Victor to do is watch people refuse to choose or to make the wrong choice. Anyone with children has experienced this. A leader must honor those who accept choice by giving them their time and effort, and resist the urge to coddle those who refuse to choose.

As Internet pornography use became more and more rampant among kids, I met with my sons and explained to them why any involvement in it was unacceptable in our family and then offered them a choice. Their mother and I were to have access to their computers and phones at all times. If we learned that they had viewed pornography in any form, they would immediately forfeit the next sports season. They would have chosen to let their teams and coaches down. Since they play three sports a year and are top players on their teams, this was a heavy responsibility to place on their shoulders. We did not plead or cajole; we explained the situation, offered a choice, and held them accountable.

Suffering vs. Pain

Avoiding choice often leads to suffering—and, ironically, making choices often brings pain. Here's what I mean: Making choices almost always results in temporary discomfort, but over time allows for direction. Avoiding choice results in discomfort over the long-term because no direction can be established. Say that you're out of shape and want to lose weight. By not choosing to get in shape, you suffer from being overweight and the consequences that go with it. By choosing to get in shape, you experience pain—the pain of working out and eating vegetables instead of hamburgers.

If my golf game can improve by sharpening my putting skills, I can choose to experience the pain of skipping some golf games in order to practice putting . . . or I can avoid choice, play the games, and suffer from a poor putting game. If my son continues to neglect his responsibility of emptying the trash, I can choose the pain of punishing him . . . or avoid choice and continue to suffer from the overflowing trashcan.

A friend of mine flew to see me in Colorado five years ago because he wanted to talk about how miserable he was in his job. At fifty years old, he'd made enough money to retire. He complained about how immoral he thought the company was. He hated going to work every day.

"What do you want to do?" I asked.

"I want to spend time with my son and raise hunting dogs," he said.

"Okay," I replied, "quit your job, raise hunting dogs, and spend more time with your son."

Then came the first excuse.

"I have a big bonus coming up in a few months," he explained. "I can't quit until then."

At that point, the conversation was effectively over. I turned the subject to baseball because what he was really stating was that he just wanted to suffer in his job instead of experience the pain of choice to leave and follow his dream. He still works at the same company. He calls every six months or so to tell me how much he hates his job.

Look at life and you see choice in everything. If you want to learn Spanish but avoid the choice of doing so, you suffer in your perceived need to know the language and your continued inability to speak it. If you choose to learn Spanish, you experience the pain of studying it.

The mother of a spoiled child suffers. She avoids taking him into public, she endures his disrespect and bad attitude, and she spends excessively to satisfy his wishes. Why? Because she doesn't want to experience the pain of punishing him in order to set firm boundaries.

There are some people who have the appearance of making a choice but actually haven't. They say they've decided to get in shape. They buy running shoes and tell all their friends. They get a DVD on running and buy a juicer and fresh vegetables. But there's always a reason they can't run, and the juicer gathers dust while the vegetables rot. Simply put, you haven't made a choice until you feel the pain of your choice. You haven't decided to get in shape until you feel the ache of running. You haven't decided to learn Spanish until you feel the pain of studying.

A reporter asked Ethiopian marathoner Abebe Bikila to describe his training regimen. The runner didn't understand the question. The reporter rephrased the question a few times until he finally just asked Mr. Bikila what he did when he ran.

"Ah," answered Bikila, "every day I find the pain, and I break it!"

The fact is, growth comes from choice, and you have only made the choice when you experience the pain of action.

Pain is weakness leaving the body.
United States Marine Corps motto

As Victors continue to make painful choices, Victims declare they have no choice, spending their lives immersed in suffering. Since Victims believe they have no choice and therefore can't improve their situation, they look to take from others.

So then we see that Victors are suffering under the tyranny of the Victims. Victors are willing to make choices—even tough ones—and endure the pain that comes with them. They are willing to delay gratification, accept hardship and hard work today for a reward tomorrow (or two years from now). Victims avoid making choices and sidestep any difficulty and discomfort, expecting instead freebies and handouts. Will we suffer in resignation or rage or will we join in a peaceful revolution by working together to take back freedom?

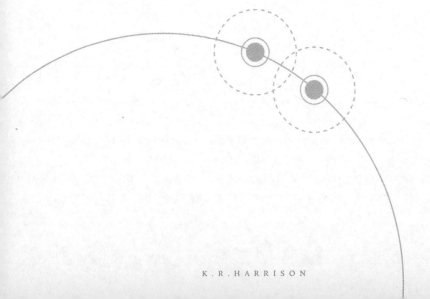

3

MANAGING CHOICE

A dead thing can go with the stream,
but only a living thing can go against it.

G. K. Chesterton

To be successful, you must manage choice. If you can't manage it in yourself, you can't manage it in others. I tell my employees that we make mutual choices about each other every day. They decide to come to work and be an employee of our company, and we decide to employ them. At any moment, either one of us can choose not to have this relationship.

They may say, "But I have no choice. I've got bills to pay, alimony, debt, and on and on." The part about having no choice is untrue and is the language of Victims. Remember, Victims declare that they have no choices. In reality, they could choose to sell their house and rent a modest apartment, or change their lifestyle to have fewer bills, or reconcile with their spouse, or live frugally and pay off their debt, or go on welfare. Maybe these choices are realistic and maybe they aren't, but these individuals make thousands of choices every day that lead them into one of our offices as an employee. When they are conscious that it is their choice to work for us, it has a positive effect on morale, even if nothing else changed. Too many people live in resentment and resignation, showing up to their job, claiming that they are forced to.

Leadership and management also choose to employ them. Management declaring they must employ people they don't want matches the number of employees who declare they have no choice. Leaders tolerate mediocrity, not understanding that their people stay employed at their choice. It is amazing how many employees I have had who I thought were irreplaceable until they needed to be replaced. In the end, it is simply laziness, fear, or indecision that leads managers to allow unproductive people to stay employed.

Think of this principle as it relates to families. Let's say your eighth-grader is at risk of failing math. He makes all kinds of excuses: "I'm just no good at math—my brain isn't wired for it . . . The teacher is too hard . . . The grading system isn't fair!"

This kid has developed a Victim mentality. Furthermore, he insists he has no choice in the matter: "There's nothing I can do! I'm stuck with this teacher and her lousy ways of teaching. All I can do is hope for the best—that she has mercy on me and lets me pass."

Of course, this child does have choices. He could ask the teacher for individual help. He could request tutoring. He could find online instructional tools. He could seek assistance from a math-proficient classmate.

The parents of this struggling student also have choices. They could leave the child to his own with well-meaning clichés like, "Try harder" and "Do the best you can." But that hands-off approach is not what Victors would do. Victor parents would offer to sit down with their child in the evening to go over the math homework together. They would help to find learning resources. They would offer strategies to improve study habits and test taking. They would choose to be as engaged and involved as possible.

Stand and Deliver

The more efficient you are, the quicker you generate choice. The person who wins the golf tournament does so because he did less than anyone on the course. A runner trains to eliminate every extra move in his stride. Don't mistake being busy for progress. In reality, you may only be busy because you are inefficient.

Ultimately, since our biology can't keep up with technology, people are being replaced. If there is a better way of getting things done than you, you will be replaced. This is why it is so important to understand what value you bring to each relationship and every transaction. You can declare it unfair, but this won't save you; and if you're honest, you will see that you do this yourself in thousands of transactions a month.

For instance, imagine that you have a favorite coffee shop where you stop every day because of the great blueberry muffins. You pass several other coffee shops on the way to this one because Steve, who owns the shop, has the best muffins. For years, you see Steve every Monday through Friday between 7:00 and 7:15. You look forward to seeing Steve and talking about the surf or the snow in the mountains or how the fishing has been.

One day, Steve announces he no longer sells the muffins. You try the other offerings, but nothing is all that good. One day, a friend takes you to Shari's Bakery, where she makes the best cinnamon rolls. Your day now starts at Shari's. So what was your relationship to Steve worth? Was it false? Did you not really care about the surf, snow, or fishing when you talked it over with him? Of course you did. Your relationship with Steve was genuine, but in the transaction part of your relationship, he could no longer deliver.

This happens in your life every day. Relationships, no matter how genuine, are based on your ability to deliver what that relationship demands. In business, you might have relationships with vendors and clients that go beyond work; your families may know each other. In the end, though, it is based on what you can deliver.

Every relationship involves this dynamic. Everyone has someone to serve and this holds true in every walk of life. In your marriage, your spouse has expectations. As a parent, your kids have expectations. To the President of the United States, the country's citizens have expectations. Ask yourself what the expectations are for you in each relationship, whether you choose to meet them, and what you are doing to meet them. Victors seek to meet the expectations in their relationships in mutually rewarding transactions. Victims seek only to take from their relationships.

A few years ago, I had lunch with the pastor of a large church. He recounted a wedding he had just officiated and said he hated doing wedding ceremonies. I thought that was a strange thing for a pastor to say, so I asked him why.

When a person takes their eyes off of fulfilling the expectations of their relationships, all they have left is self-preservation.
John Cundiff

"Because I've been doing them for so long that I can tell what the marriage will be like just from looking in their eyes," he answered. "So many people look at each other and their eyes say, 'Wow, are you going to make me happy!' They have absolutely no sense of what their spouse wants and often don't care. They're just looking to take, and it's never really hit them that marriage is all about giving."

Sadly, what he was describing were two Victims who had just found each other. Or worse, a Victim had found a Victor.

The Nature of Transactions

All transactions require mutual satisfaction. When you purchased the cinnamon roll from Shari, she required you to pay her stated price, and you required her to provide a cinnamon roll that met your expectations. This is a Victor transaction and involves choice. At its base level, we see a Victim in the transaction as a shoplifter, who steals the cinnamon roll. He has satisfied his need by taking, but he has not satisfied the other side of the transaction by paying. He has sought to be served in the transaction but not offered to serve.

Transactions or exchanges occur continuously in all areas of life. Family, friends, vendors, and co-workers—everyone is constantly reassessing each other's ability to perform in a mutually rewarding transaction. This is how so many marriages decline in

time. One or both partners fail to continually adapt in order to behave in a mutually rewarding way. Thus, resentment takes hold.

We learn this in infancy: "Give me a bottle, and I'll give you
peace and quiet." We learn to use this transaction to our advantage and become comfortable with this system until the first
time it doesn't work. Mom says no, and our comfortable system
breaks down. You can see the confusion on a toddler's face as she
enters her Terrible Twos. She concludes that maybe if she does
what worked before with more enthusiasm, she'll get what she
wants. So she throws herself on the ground and begins to scream.

Her first conscious learning begins as she sees whether doing
what worked before gets her what she wants. If she's punished,
she learns that she must learn a new way to win in her transaction. If she's appeased, she learns that in a tantrum if she just did
what she did before (cry) louder and longer, she'll get her way.

There are four fundamental stages of a transaction's life cycle: identity, relationship, value, and choice. It is useful to understand that if people don't choose, it is because they don't see
the value in a transaction. If they don't see the value, it's because
there is a lack of relationship. If there is a lack of relationship, it's
because a sufficient identity has yet to be established.

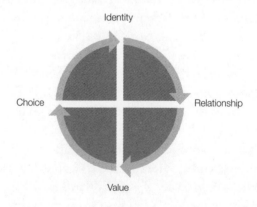

Search for Identity

We're all involved in a quest for identity. Everyone gets their identity from somewhere. People either create their own identity or it is imposed upon them. It can be self-generated, come from other sources, such as relationships, profession, education, or reputation. Their primary identity will come from being an athlete, a mom, an intellectual, a doctor, a liberal, a Christian, a leader, an African-American, a Michigan Wolverine, a Marine, a Harvard graduate, a bully, a musician—it can come from a myriad of things.

Notice that some identities are self-created and some come from belonging to a group. Some people are aware of their identity and their actions are consistent with it, but most are not. When someone hasn't created their own identity, it is imposed on them. This can cause untold stress on a person, as imposed identities are often inconsistent with who or what they think they actually are, but they have no identity to counter it. This is seen in an obvious sense in the angst exhibited by so many teenagers. They join clubs, teams, and cliques, seeking identity and affirmation from the outside.

Adults who have no knowledge or control of their identity end up filled with confusion and resentment, but they learn to cover it more successfully as they get older. They use phrases like, "I need to find myself" or "I need to find out who I am." Really, they are saying that their identity has been imposed upon them from the outside, and they are unable to create their own. They live life in confusion, being offended often and contributing rarely, because as they enter into the transactions of the day, they have no idea what their offer is.

When you need a heart transplant, you don't look for the cheapest price, you look for identity. Think of a surgeon who shows you his wide array of degrees, describes the procedure in detail to you and impresses you with all he knows. He tells you that your chances of successful recovery are X percent, if the following things don't happen. Compare that surgeon to one who has a great reputation, greets you with a handshake, and says with a wink, "I've done this procedure more times than I can remember. You're going to be fine." Who gives you more confidence? Experts project identity; they don't explain themselves.

Offense comes when we violate someone's perceived identity. Take a college professor and tell him that you don't think he's very athletic and odds are he won't care. Tell him he's not very bright, and you offend him terribly. Take someone whose identity is being an athlete and say the same thing, and you will get a different reaction. The difference is each person's identity.

I was in a restaurant in Birmingham, Alabama, when my waitress told me she was working over the summer but would be going back to school. I asked her if she went to the University of Auburn, and she was terribly offended. "Of course not!" she said indignantly, "I go to Alabama!" I had inadvertently violated her identity. Roll Tide.

Some people generate identity from within and some seek theirs from the outside. When some people walk into a room, they say, "Here I am!" This means, they bring their identity with them and demand others recognize it. When others walk into a room, they say, "Where are you?" This means, they gain their identity by who they surround themselves with.

My wife was the consummate businesswoman. She rose through the ranks at a national jewelry chain and by the time she was 25, she was running the most profitable district in the company. As the only district manager who was not a man in his forties, this attracted a lot of attention.

Her identity was professional in every way, and she had little interest in children. If we went to a party and there was a dog and a baby, she would spend time playing with the dog and not even notice the baby. When she got pregnant, she had to take maternity leave early due to medical issues. The person running the district in her absence failed and profit margins dipped. My wife struggled as she watched her financials diminish, and she couldn't wait to have the baby so she could get back to work.

Then she gave birth. A week after our daughter was born, my wife said she didn't want to go back to work. Seeing our daughter, she realized she never wanted to leave her. She said, "I just want to be a mom." Our baby grew into a high school girl whose friends now know my wife as Super Mom. They flock to our house and seek her advice on everything from hygiene to religion to relationships. People who have only known her in the past 15 to 20 years can't believe there was ever a time she wasn't passionate about children. She chose to change her identity from super professional to super mom in order to form an offer, which in this case was to raise a child.

What Do You Have to Offer?

Your offer is a promise to the future that is a manifestation of your intention. When people are not clear about their offer or their identity, they expect others to be responsible for it. The offer is always changing to meet the demands in which you are involved, but the intention does not. You have dignity when your offers are consistently coherent. For instance, a young husband's intention is to provide for his family. In early marriage, this may result in an offer to work long hours to build a financial foundation for his growing family. Later, his offer may need to change to working less in order to coach Little League or help his wife through a hard time. In both cases, the intention is the same—to provide for his family. The offer changes in ways that consistently align with his intention. The first offer is to provide for the most pressing need—finances. The second offer provides for the needs at that time: involvement with growing children or emotional support for a wife in distress.

In order for us to make an offer to someone, we must identify that person's concern and decide if we choose to offer a solution. Ask yourself, "To what concern and in what community do I offer to be a solution?" As an offer is distilled, conditions of satisfaction become clear and the relationships narrow accordingly.

Conditions of satisfaction are not an offer. They are what is required to deliver on an offer. The offer and conditions of satisfaction must be measurable by money, time, actions, or other specific means. For instance, a woman may decide that what she wants in a potential husband is someone who is adventurous, wants to see the world, and loves challenges. If a man who wants to date her has an offer of stability and financial security but not adventure, she will likely choose not to participate in his offer.

Notice the importance of having a clear identity before making an offer. One without the other is worthless:

Offer without identity = Slavery
Identity without offer = Arrogance
Identity + offer = Successful relationships

Those who make an offer without a clear identity are destined to spend their lives being taken advantage of again and again. This is because they have not formed who they are and their standards for mutual contribution in a transaction. Those who have an identity with no offer are simply arrogant. Have you noticed how many people seem to be completely arrogant with no apparent reason to be? It's because they have formed an identity in their own minds with no basis in reality. They do not seek to be a solution to anyone's concerns but their own.

When the Continental Congress met to decide who would lead the army against the British, they had two offers: John Hancock or George Washington. Hancock had a clear identity as the richest man in the colonies, but his identity was limited to that. His self-importance is evident if you look at the Declaration of Independence where all of the signatories, such as Benjamin Franklin and Thomas Jefferson, are small and in neat rows, while Hancock's is centered below them all and much larger. His arrogance led him to make an offer to lead the army without an identity to be able to do so. Washington, meanwhile, wore his British officer's uniform to the meeting and was overwhelmingly voted to be America's first general. Washington, D.C., has great monuments to George Washington and Thomas Jefferson. However, if you want to see a monument to John Hancock, you will have to travel to a small graveyard in Boston to view it.

If you have no identity, you can originate no credible offer. You become a Victim, because you're forced to be reactive in transactions rather than proactive. In the end, all Victims have only one offer. It comes in a thousand different forms, but they're all really the same: "I'm here to demand that you take care of me." They're everywhere you look: in cubicles, eating at the breakfast table, driving a police car, waiting on your table, even sleeping next to you. In every transaction, they have only one goal—to assuage their ego and make themselves comfortable. They resist discomfort or humiliation at all costs. Because learning can only come with some degree of discomfort and humiliation, they can't grow.

The Appeal of Authenticity

Your offer and your identity must be authentic to be accepted or you will be revealed as a fraud. Who you are will expose itself in a moment of panic. Many people who are fatigued, stressed, anxious, or out-of-sorts act in a way that they claim "isn't them." I submit to you that it is *exactly* them. In fact, it's more them then when they have it all together. How we act when we aren't composed enough to put on our daily survival act exposes who we are.

Be more concerned with your character than your reputation,
because your character is what you really are,
while your reputation is merely what others think you are.

John Wooden

A famous celebrity was involved in a hit-and-run accident in Los Angeles a few years ago. She ran a red light and left the other driver with a broken arm and in need of stitches. When she was arrested the next day, she claimed that she wasn't a criminal; she simply panicked. She couldn't understand what people were upset about.

What she failed to realize was that her actions in her moment of panic revealed who she was. The woman in the other car was injured but might have been dying, for all the celebrity knew, as she fled the scene. Rather than worry about another human life or her own character, she worried about lawsuits and her reputation.

Contrast this incident with an illegal alien who ran a red light and hit my grandmother as she crossed the street. The car wasn't moving very fast, but she became stuck under the bumper. The driver stopped immediately and helped her, calling an ambulance. He had no driver's license and no insurance, and said later that he thought the police would throw him in prison for the rest of his life. Even though he thought this, in his moment of panic he stopped and helped the person he hurt. Ironically, had he fled, he would have run her over and killed her, and would indeed have gone to prison. As it was, my grandmother suffered a broken collarbone and nothing more.

Who you are, the choices you have made over a lifetime, and the stories you do or don't have are all revealed in the unguarded moments. In a crisis, is your immediate response to be defensive? Is it to formulate a story about why it isn't your fault? Is it to blame someone else? Or is it to take responsibility and to learn?

Crises and confrontations are learning moments, and Victors use them to further their growth and increase their opportunities.

4

AMBITION:
THE ART OF AIMING HIGH

Luck is what happens when preparation meets opportunity.

Seneca, Roman philosopher

When I switched from a small Christian high school to a large public school, I assumed I would start for their basketball team the way I always had. However, I had no idea what their needs were or how I fit into the team. In other words, I had no identity or offer of how to be a contribution to their intention of winning basketball games. I expected to be a starter because that's what I had been previously and that's what I wanted. The first game of the season, I played for a total of fifty seconds.

I went home that night and was forced to be honest about my abilities. I couldn't shoot or dribble and wasn't particularly coordinated—not a great profile for a varsity basketball player. What I could do was jump and outmuscle people. I realized at that moment that the only contribution I could really make to the team was as a "garbage" player—a physical player known for rebounding. Unknowingly, I formed an identity that night, as a power player who would go after every loose ball, set hard screens, and play aggressive defense. The next day at practice, a new player stepped onto the court. By the end of the season, I was MVP of the team and combing through college basketball scholarship offers.

I was ambitious about playing basketball. You could say that I knew what I wanted and went out and took it. That isn't right, however. That's what I did to begin with and ended up sitting on the bench. What I did to end up being a starter was to figure out what my offer was in order to contribute to the team.

The Victim definition of ambition is "knowing what you want and getting it." At first glance, this sounds right. Most people go through life with this understanding. The problem is, of course, that there is no basic understanding of the needs of others in this definition. One becomes emotionally tied to the insistence that others take his/her offer because it helps them get what they want. Take it far enough, and dishonesty and deception eventually rule. Why would you sacrifice for "the right thing to do" when this doesn't get you to your ambition?

The Victor definition of ambition is "knowing who you are and giving it." Say you are an ambitious plumber. Your offer may be cheap and fast plumbing services. People know they'll get a quick fix, cheaply, but if there are bigger issues, they need to call someone else. Or your offer may be comprehensive, highly skilled plumbing work, but expensive. People know that you will solve all of their plumbing needs, but it will cost them. In the case of either offer, you're offering what you are and others can decide if that's what they want.

What is Starbucks' identity? They are a worldwide chain of chic coffee shops. What's their offer? It is good, expensive coffee, served quickly. When you see Starbucks, you know their identity and their offer. No matter whether you're in Manhattan or Barstow, that offer will be consistent. It's your choice whether their identity attracts you and whether you choose to participate in their offer.

Notice in the proper ambition/offer definition, there is no need for coercion, dishonesty, or manipulation. What is required is simply the flexibility to provide what is needed in a particular relationship. This is why the railroads don't own the airlines. They thought they were in the railroad business and didn't realize they were in the transportation business. As people's needs shifted to mass air travel, the railroads persisted in an offer that no longer had the same demand.

One can see this dilemma in the family when the children leave home. Too often, one or both parents have become vested in their identities to their children and no longer have an offer to each other as spouses. As the "Empty Nest Syndrome" sets in, many couples do not shift their identities to be an offer to their spouse's concerns, and the family breaks apart.

Go Before You Know

The more prepared you are, the more quickly you can make a choice. John Cundiff tells the story of touring construction sites in Phoenix in the 1980s with a major developer. The developer asked questions of several construction workers and was impressed with one of them. At the end of the tour, he asked the foreman to send in the young man to talk. He offered the young man a job and told him he could start immediately. The worker said he would think about it. As the developer left, the foreman asked him if he wanted the young man's contact information.

"No," he said, "he made his choice already."

Contrast this with the story of a young corporal in Napoleon's army. Napoleon loved strong, beautiful horses. The one he was riding got spooked and began to buck. The men around him watched as Napoleon tried in vain to control the horse. Suddenly, a corporal stepped forward, risking his life, and grabbed the reins. When he had controlled the horse, he handed the reins back to Napoleon.

"Nice work . . . Captain," the emperor said to the young corporal.

Startled, the corporal asked, "Captain of what?"

"Captain of my Private Guard," Napoleon answered.

The young man immediately ripped the corporal stripes from his uniform and walked up the hill, throwing his musket to the ground (French officers didn't carry muskets). When he got to the Private Guard without the proper insignias or officer's uniform, the officers asked him what he thought he was doing. He said he was the new Captain of the Private Guard.

"By whose orders?" they asked.

"By the order of the emperor!" he said, and immediately took command.

He didn't apologize for his youth or lack of credentials, nor did he stop to consider their feelings. He didn't think about politics or what people would say about him. He seized his opportunity. The emperor declared him a captain, and he immediately started acting like a captain. He didn't have the training, education, or social standing to be a captain, but when his opportunity came, he was ready.

Those whose identity and offer is clear are ready to grasp opportunity when it comes. A friend of mine was the CEO of Rentrak Corporation. Rentrak had developed the technology in the late '80s that allowed video stores to go from having a handful of new releases to having a wall full of them. They did this by developing a process where, instead of buying the movies, the stores could rent them by giving the movie studios a cut of each rental, thereby keeping overhead down.

I'm a great believer in luck, and I find
the harder I work the more I have of it.
Thomas Jefferson

In the early 2000s, my friend saw that technology was going to make movie rental stores obsolete, so he developed a data tracking technology to meet the changing demands of his customers.

"I saw that the ratings system for television was too vague," he told me. "Networks could ascertain that X amount of women between seventeen and thirty-five watched a TV show, but that was all. Who were these women? Were they married? Single mothers? Black? White? What products did they buy? I knew that if I could get advertisers specific data like this, it would be invaluable. So I started developing the software that could track this information ten years ago. I had no idea where we'd get the data, but I gambled that the same technology that would eventually dry up our video business would provide us with the data."

He was right. Just as Rentrak's foundational business was going the way of the typewriter, the company's stock went from $2.00 per share to $60.00. Victors, who have honed their identity and know their offer to a specific concern, are prepared to go before they are completely certain of the outcome, confident in their preparation.

Ready to Risk

People avoid choice and therefore opportunity because it involves risk. Many people are obsessed with avoiding risk. They review, assess, and evaluate incessantly in order to avoid choice. This is a Victim mentality that breaks down the ability to make decisions.

Victims believe that risk is variable and they are the constant. This causes some people to obsess on analysis, trying in vain to find the magic pill that removes all risk. Victors inherently know that risk is constant and people are the only variable. A common belief is that people can minimize risk by altering circumstances or situations. This leads to the habit of developing plans that are only solutions to previous problems. A proper approach accepts that risk is a constant and that the only variable is people. This makes people accountable for their own futures and not victims of circumstances.

Risk impacts biology. This reaction is immediately interpreted in language as emotions. These emotions trigger our survival habits of action. When observed over time, these recurring interpretations and actions can be seen as a person's history.

All organisms, when faced with actual or perceived risk, respond with one of four survival strategies: dictate, migrate, tolerate, or hibernate. They do this in an attempt to control an outcome based on their primary concern: certainty, freedom, stability, or security. Most people have a distinctive reaction in an emergency consistent with one of these four concerns.

Remember the story that started this chapter? There was risk in making an offer to be a physical, "garbage" player. Based on the concern for certainty, how could I know the team wanted a garbage player? What if they rejected the offer and I lost the fifty seconds of playing time I had been getting? Based on a concern for freedom, if I established an identity as a garbage player, would I be locked into that role?

Concerning stability, the next day at practice I got in a fight with the star player who was bigger than me. He didn't appreciate the way I slammed into him and ripped the ball away from him. So there was a risk to my popularity, as well as a concern for my security. That player insisted the coach kick me off the team and ultimately he quit the team because I took his starting position.

This simple story illustrates the foundational principle that in order to fulfill the ambition for success in any relationship, from fitting into a sports team to having a successful marriage, one must develop an identity that has an offer to be a contribution in that relationship. This will always have risk; the only constant is you.

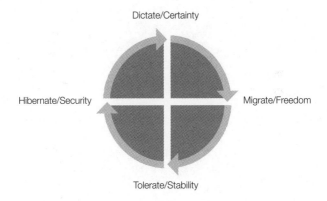

5

THE LANGUAGE OF LEADERSHIP

Compromise is what people do when they lose sight
of their own ability to determine the future.

John Cundiff

One of the foundational declarations of Victims is that someone else is in charge. Victors understand that they are "in charge"
of everything for which they are responsible.

A young woman making coffee drinks at her local coffee
shop is in the leadership capacity for how her drinks turn out.
A Victor understands that only she is responsible for whether her
customers will have an excellent experience in the aspects that
have to do with her. She is the leader in those transactions and
their success is largely dependent on her.

Leadership is the daily battleground between chaos and
control. It happens in many transactions each day to all of us,
whether we're interacting with our children, the mail carrier, or
a staff of hundreds. This leadership capacity can't be summoned
at the moment of crisis if it has been squandered by years of compromise. Compromise is what people do when they lose sight
of their own ability to determine the future. When someone is
dedicated to his or her intention, there is no compromise.

People point to qualities such as skill, talent, charisma,
and enthusiasm in an attempt to identify the core elements of
leadership. Notice that these are just the symptoms of the more
fundamental personal commitment to give rather than receive
assurance about the future in the midst of crisis. This conviction
to speak in the moment without doubt or compromise gives assurance to others and refocuses attention on action now rather
than the reasons why not from the past.

There is no more basic example of leadership than a mother.
She will not compromise the safety of her child; she is clear on
her intention to love and protect her child, no matter what the
crisis. An effective mother is constantly in the battleground of
chaos and control, and her best tool is giving her child assurance
about the future. "Mommy will kiss the scrape on your knee,
and it will get better." Her assurance is only effective if she has
developed trust by being accountable in her duties to her child.

Corrie ten Boom is one of the heroes of World War II. She and her sister were caught hiding Jews from the Nazis and sent to a concentration camp. As Corrie suffered through the torture, humiliation, and starvation, her sister encouraged her and kept her alive. After years of imprisonment, they were shifted to a different camp and as they crawled into the straw bunks that made up their new sleeping quarters, fleas attacked them by the millions. Corrie began to despair as she was nearing the end of her ability to hope. As she looked at her sister, she saw she was smiling and asked her why. She said she was grateful for the fleas.

Corrie was incredulous, but her sister simply said that since all things worked together for good for God's people, the fleas must be there for a reason. A few days later, the prisoners asked the guards to come into their room to settle a dispute, but they refused because of the fleas. After that, the prisoners realized they had the freedom, for the first time in years, to speak and plan free from the guards. In a moment of chaos, Corrie's sister gave, rather than sought, assurance about the future.

Worry does not empty tomorrow of its sorrow,
it empties today of its strength.

Corrie ten Boom

Many people compromise their future in uncertain or risky circumstances. They believe that until they have assurance about the future outcome they cannot focus on contributing to those around them. This habit promotes lowered expectations and leads to denial that a crisis even exists. In this condition, people are blind to the realization that contributing to others in a crisis is the only way of determining the outcome. In other words, the only solution to anxiety and uncertainty is contribution.

Victors promote mutual contribution as the only solution to anxiety in times of crisis. A leader's job is to create the assurance necessary for others to find the courage to make the choice to participate fully in determining the outcome. This can only be accomplished by maintaining a relentless focus on the end in mind without compromise. This is a Victor's true contribution and can only be achieved by people with the courage to initiate the natural process of accomplishment rather than focusing on the individual concerns of those involved.

A friend called me recently to complain that his son, a freshman in high school, was getting poor grades because of a lack of ambition. His son was smart but simply wouldn't put out the effort. I told him that I had a similar problem with one of my kids a few years ago. I didn't address the problem at all. Instead, I drove all three of my kids to a rundown neighborhood in Los Angeles. We drove around for fifteen minutes and then I pulled to the curb in front of some dilapidated houses.

"Look around, kids," I said. "I want you to understand something. You live in a nice area because your mother and I worked hard. You are making the choices now that determine where and how you will live when you're adults. If you work hard, you'll have the choice to live where we live. If you don't, your choices are limited to living in a place like this. Your mother and I can't make those choices for you. You make them every day, and they determine your future."

All three kids' grades improved after that, and we've revisited that moment a few times since then when we needed to. I summed up the story for my friend: "Your son doesn't understand that he lives where he does and has the lifestyle he has because of *your* hard work. He's not *entitled* to it. You as his leader need to make him understand that his future is based on choices made by him, not entitlements given by you."

Leadership is the capacity to create a vacuum that attracts contribution by others, and removes anxiety in the moment of crisis. The ability to convey assurance and manifest conviction is what calls other people to action. You can't push people anymore effectively than you can push water. To move water or people, you must create a vacuum. In leadership, this is done by properly identifying the issue or problem without judgment and speaking in a way that conveys certainty about the outcome. This allows committed people to support each other with actions that help determine the outcome rather than fall into uncertainty and negativity.

When faced with a crisis situation, people fall into one of two categories: those who seek assurance and those who give it. The choice to give or seek assurance in crisis is rarely a conscious decision on the part of an individual, but the consequences of this choice will determine the viability of a person's leadership success.

Leaders with the capacity to convey assurance about the outcome in crisis will also notice that they are attracting Victors who seek the opportunity to participate in determining a new future, rather than becoming distracted by Victims wanting more assurance before they consider participating. Victors want the opportunity, not the explanation, and know that contributing to the collective effort will ultimately resolve the crisis. This begins to build a cycle of conviction and confidence manifested by a self-determining team.

Truth or Consequences

The most important trait of a true leader is the ability to separate truth from lies. Truth always demands a hearing. It demands to be exposed and refuses to stay covered up. It doesn't ask to be tolerated. It simply is. Truth says, "Shine a light on me, and I will be evident." Truth says that if you jump off the Chrysler Building in New York, you will die. Gravity will make you fall. There is no argument, no gray area.

Lies, exaggerations, and gossip demand tolerance. They're secretive and whisper behind closed doors. Their biggest demand is that things are relative, that the facts can sway based on perceptions. Lies, exaggerations, and gossip insist that everything falls into shades of gray, with no black and white. "The truth is all in your perspective. If you insist on only one set of facts, you are narrow-minded."

Notice that if you jump from the Chrysler Building, it will be immediately evident that truth is black and white. Your perspective doesn't matter, there is no gray area, you will fall and you will die. When faced with a crisis, the clarity of truth is obvious. All the nonsense about gray area and relativity disappears.

The further society drifts from the truth,
the more it will hate those that speak it.

George Orwell

Victims hate truth. Truth not only demands to be exposed, but it is also the great exposer. It is a light on every situation, and it exposes Victims. The time Victors spend on progress, Victims spend on surviving. Depending on their intelligence and cunning, they become adept at manipulating leaders who don't understand their own identity and offer.

Humility

I've heard it said many times that anyone who thinks he or she can be president of the United States must be arrogant to think they can do the job. When you hear statements like this, it is simply Victims declaring themselves. Any student of history knows that many of the greatest presidents were very humble. Abraham

Lincoln was notorious for his meekness and modesty. Calvin Coolidge, one of the most underrated presidents in history, was renown for never talking about himself.

A friend of mine was a three-star admiral at Bethesda Hospital when President Reagan was brought in after being shot. He tells of seeing the president near death when he got there and had only just been stabilized. When no one was around, the President got up to get himself some water and dropped the cup, spilling water. A nurse came into the room to find him on his knees, wiping the water from the floor. Horrified, she told him she would wipe up the water and grabbed some towels. Reagan just smiled at her and said, "That's okay, I'm the one who spilled it."

There is no correlation between someone's ability to lead and their ego. Just as there are incompetent fools who are arrogant, there are amazing leaders who are filled with humility. Victims assume leaders are arrogant because they can't understand a person's ability to take a stand and point the way forward. Victims try to tear down heroes. They've rewritten the stories of George Washington, Abraham Lincoln, Theodore Roosevelt, and other great American leaders through their lens of cynicism to cope with their own ineptitude. They are offended by greatness because it shines a light on their emptiness.

Victims demand that you apologize for being a leader. Their thinking is that if you believe you have the skills to do the job, you must be arrogant. This is the thinking of people who refuse to choose, screaming offense at the possibility of greatness in others. Too many true leaders are afraid to claim their natural place at the helm of society because they see the Victims lined up to destroy anyone who dares to point toward the future.

The fact is, there are people who are gifted at being leaders, and there is nothing arrogant about using those gifts. We need them more than ever in this generation. We need people with vision and conviction to point the way and to pull in those around them to whom they can hand those ideas. The erosion of the foundation of our society is due in part to the lack of people willing to participate. The foundational interdependence is still strong in the American people, but we need true leaders to step forward and say "I."

Notice that being a Victor or Victim has nothing to do with being a leader or follower. Often we assume that the most talented people are always leaders. Not so. Leadership is a talent, no different from musical ability, athleticism, or natural intelligence. However, because we need true leaders to step forward, we must understand the distinction between Victor leaders who can create the space for further growth, and Victim leaders who will destroy creativity and stagnate us further.

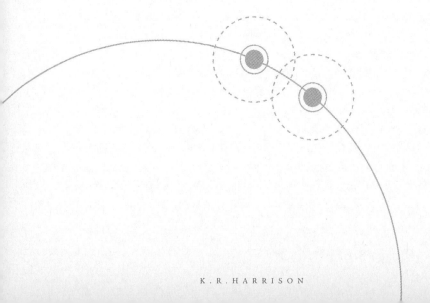

6

VICTIMS IN LIFE

Some people aren't used to an environment
where excellence is expected.

Steve Jobs

As we grow up, one way we get to know ourselves is by reading the expressions on other people's faces. All our lives, those of us with courage have learned we must stand up straight and say, "Pick me!" When this performance fails to produce a positive result from others, Victims take refuge in ironic cynicism as protection.

Cynicism requires detachment and a pretense of superiority. Most important, cynicism and irony require a complete removal of passion. This allows the practitioners to dismiss the negative reaction and disapproval of others with a grin and a shrug. Irony and cynicism protect them from having to reflect on their impact on others. This is why we see so many leaders presiding over failed policies and hurt people with no pretense of responsibility. They have a long list of others who are responsible for the failures, even when they are the ones in charge.

A man who had been a football coach for three years but won only one game said to me, "Yeah, if I could only get the right players!" As he shook his head and wore his best Victim facial expression, I could see in his eyes that he really believed it. That his losing teams might be his responsibility had never occurred to him.

Lacking competence at managing their own identity, Victims have designed a system that attacks all threats to their presumed superiority. They have devised an educational system that instills the soft contempt of lowered expectation that teaches our children to dream of becoming famous for being famous. No need to contribute to others by learning to develop integrity and character, because that has all been replaced by brittle doctrine. Even if you resisted this thinking, your children's teachers might not have.

The consequence is that we have lost the capacity to model and provide access to the fundamentals of character. Victims have encouraged our culture's fascination with personal rights and entitlements. This is bankrupting our nation due to the unsustainable costs. We have been told that until everyone has the political right to personal recognition and that everyone is exceptional, no individual can be a winner. No group can possibly be exceptional until every individual is. So we tell our children that no one actually won the soccer game, otherwise one team would have lost, and we can't have that.

A lie is an act of self-abdication, because one surrenders one's reality to the person to whom one lies, making that person one's master.

Ayn Rand

This has jammed our culture with sensitivity training and political correctness, and the massive overhead cost of government enforcement. The concern for personal rights and entitlements has made our culture too timid and slow to respond to the ruthless, unmerciful demands of our modern world.

When we confuse our identity with our ego, everything becomes about what "I" think, believe, or feel, and if "I" am not validated, you will suffer the consequences. "I know my rights and what I'm entitled to; please alert Human Resources and my lawyer." This worldview invalidates Victors who may still have the passion and ambition to consider what others think, feel, and believe, and offers a solution to their problems based on truth.

The ultimate consequence of this rights and entitlement fantasy is extreme cynicism and bitterness. It is a very short trip to the next stop, which is government intervention and outright takeover of our freedoms. Victims, who are unable to separate individual ego from a managed identity, are actively eliminating Victors from key roles in organizations.

The Victims' Version

Victims develop their own meanings for words, seeking to use the morals of Victors against them. Words that have true meaning are distorted and set up as a means to demand that Victors defend themselves for their crime of ambition. Words like *judgment, greed, hypocrisy* and *racism* are set up as false shields for Victims to avoid accountability.

Victims are liars. They lie to themselves most often, perfecting the art of telling themselves how valuable they are and how amazing they could have been if someone would have just given them a chance. They lie to others primarily to convince themselves. They are toxic to any organization, from families to countries. Some of a Victim's favorite phrases include . . .

"Don't judge me." To truly pass judgment on someone is to assign motives to their actions or criticize them without fully understanding the situation. Victims, however, distort the word "judgment" to mean any kind of assertion that they disagree with. For instance, if you catch someone in a lie and call him a liar, you are not judging him, you are simply saying what is. If someone is caught stealing and you call her a thief, you are not passing judgment, you are stating what she is.

I overheard one of my daughter's friends on the telephone with her mother while she was in our house. She told her mother she was at work. When she hung up, I asked her why she lied.

"Don't judge me," she said.

"I'm not judging you," I replied. "I'm observing that you're a liar. I have said nothing about your reasons for being one. I don't allow liars in my house, however, so call your mother back and tell her the truth or please leave."

She left.

Victims live in fear of having their compromise revealed. They live in denial and resent anyone who reminds them of their true self. Therefore, anyone who points out the truth is branded with the intolerable label of being judgmental.

"Wall Street is greedy." One can substitute any successful person or institution for "Wall Street." In the language of Victims, "greedy" means you haven't given them what they demand. Greed is taking from others in order to spend it on one's own comfort, like a small business owner who pays employees less than they've earned, or a king who overtaxes his people. Victims distort greed to condemn people who enjoy the benefits of what they've earned. Victims refuse to acknowledge the risk, work, and sacrifice that an entrepreneur endures on the way to success. They show up when success is complete, demanding that the successful "pay their fair share!" When the entrepreneur refuses, they shout, "Greed!"

"I'm offended." Victims are addicted to believing the façade rather than reality. They would rather live in their fantasy than face things as they actually are. They resent anyone who tells them the truth. This is why they are so easily offended by truth. When struck by an irrefutable fact, their retort is usually to shut down the discussion by accusing you of insensitivity. Since you are offensive, they don't need to deal with the facts. At some point, they'll usually tell you, "It isn't what you said, it's how you said it." Until you learn to say it in a way that is acceptable to them, your truth means nothing.

"The church is full of hypocrites." Of course it is. There is not another organization in America that attracts more Victims than the church. Walk into any church and the leadership will tell you that it's the same 10 percent of the people who work in the nursery, teach Sunday school, clean up after services, or work in the kitchen at social events. These are the Victors, who are there to grow as human beings. The other 90 percent are Victims, who come to church when it's convenient and are always filled with ideas about what could be done better and what's wrong with the pastor. Other Victims come to the church, see the 90 percent, and leave complaining. The church is declining in the Western

world because there are too few Victors to support the Victims that fill its buildings.

Victims breed more Victims, which is why the above statements sound so commonplace. Just look at any ghetto in the world from Paris to Hong Kong to Los Angeles, and you will find mass populations who have been programmed from birth to explain why it's not their fault and if someone would just give them enough money, they could be happy.

My best advice to those who intend to become successful future leaders is that when they come to kill you, don't be there.

John Cundiff

John's quote, directly above, means that we must not fight Victims on their own terrain. They have spent their life learning to fight in the one area they know and they are experts at pulling people there. Naïve Victors think that if they can just reason with Victims and show them a better way, they can change them. In these conversations, Victims demand answers and tell their stories, stumbling toward inevitable failure and then assigning blame. In fact, all that happens to Victors who fight Victims on their own terrain is exhaustion and resignation, which can lead to bitterness.

Victims can't fight in the arenas of truth or ideas; they want to have conversations about rights and blame. This is simple to understand—it's what they spend their time thinking about. Victims are only interested in being right; they don't want to be confused with the truth. Therefore, it is important not to engage them on their grounds. Too often Victors get sucked into Victim conversations and their own momentum gets stopped.

Victims project language and attitudes of poverty, rather than prosperity. One Victim can have a remarkably negative affect on a lot of good people. A friend of mine complained that he was constantly being taken advantage of in his chiropractic business. He had set up a program where patients could pay a monthly fee and use his services as often as they needed. By the time he came to me in exasperation, he had a huge number of people who were getting free service. They had come to him saying they couldn't afford the fee but needed treatment. There were so many that his business was failing because he didn't have time for paying customers. My friend would give them a break for a few months to help them out. When one of these patients, who came five times a week, missed an entire week, my friend asked him why he had missed. "Oh," he said, "I took my family to Disneyland for the week." Others came to their appointments in new cars or bragged about things they bought.

I asked him if most of his patients left after he gave them a few months for free.

"Yes!" he said. "Once it's time for them to pay again, they just disappear."

He was afraid to confront anyone because he didn't want to be accused of being "greedy." I explained to him that it was nothing personal, and he hadn't been rejected. They just went in search of someone else to victimize.

I explained to my friend that he was attracting Victims in droves. He was desperate to demonstrate his sincerity to his customers, sacrificing constantly, without even being aware of it. His unwillingness to say no was because of false mercy. He thought that if he sacrificed, the hollow relationship would be maintained. He was also afraid of criticism. Unconsciously, he had developed unhealthy defense habits toward Victims because they had learned how to attack him to get what they want. At some point in his past, he refused to give false mercy and someone (probably a friend or family member) told him he was greedy or heartless or they simply ended the relationship.

It was painful, and he doesn't want to feel that again. So he suffers through growing waves of demands for free service, to avoid the pain of their accusations. What he fails to realize is that Victims will keep demanding their rights, until someone says, "Enough!"

All Victims are also Victimizers. They are like predators, and they have honed their skills to look for people to take care of them. They are merciless and have no capacity to see what they cost those they take from. Like parasites, they see the world as their host and they take what they can. If you were to point this out to them, they would be deeply offended because they are addicted to their habit. They aren't interested in your assessments of them or how they can improve.

Character from Within

Values are externally imposed; character is internally exposed. When politicians speak of imposing values on others, they are declaring themselves as Victims. They want to force others to reflect their own beliefs. Victors understand that it is character that comes from within and is revealed in moments of crisis. When a person is willing to take ownership of their strength they can develop the capacity to generate a powerful social identity, which is a manifestation of character.

When you are willing to stand in the face of the anxiety of others and negotiate without compromise, you will be viewed as a threat. People who have subordinated their strength and compromised their character out of anxiety about the future will never blame themselves. In order to alleviate this trend, we must come together as interdependent teams.

As I have spoken on this subject, many people have voiced concern about whether they are Victims. The answer is a relatively easy one. As we've seen, Victims are liars, those they lie to with

the greatest effectiveness is themselves, and they are constantly on
the lookout for who will contribute to them rather than to whom
they can contribute. Jesus said there are four kinds of people who
hear the truth:

(1) those who reject it;
(2) those who receive it until difficulties arise and then forget it;
(3) those who receive it until anxiety chokes it out of them;
(4) those who accept it and are productive.

Remember that Victors have an identity and an offer, which they
bring with conditions of mutual satisfaction. Victims have only an
offer and its always they same—that you take care of them. I often
answer the question about whether one is a Victim with two questions. First, is this a question that you ponder carefully, mulling it
over and considering its applicability to you, or will you soon forget
it? Second, do you approach new relationships, transactions, and
situations with an offer to help, encourage, and contribute, or do
you instead look at what you can take with no understanding of
what you can give?

I have continued to repeat that Victors give with a condition of
mutual satisfaction because I find Victors are so often manipulated
by Victims' demands that they sacrifice. A man from my church,
who I barely knew, once asked me to lunch. He informed me that
he wanted to use my company's services and asked how much they
would be for him. When I gave him the price he said, "That's what
your office told me but I thought, you know, since we both go to
the same church, you'd give me a better price."

"Why would you think that?" I asked.

"Well, we should sacrifice for each other," he said.

I just smiled. "How were you planning to sacrifice for me?"
I asked. When I saw his blank stare I said, "I was thinking that in the

spirit of sacrifice, you'd pay more." He didn't get the humor, and I paid the check.

It is important to remember that while Victims only take (or manipulate by giving only in order to take), Victors don't only give. Victors give with conditions of mutual satisfaction. Victors give and allow others to give back.

7

VICTORS IN LIFE

Motivation is simple. You eliminate those who are not motivated.

Lou Holtz

On a hot summer night while I was on the LAPD, my partner, John, and I heard an eruption of sound that we knew too well. It was a car exploding into another, leaving broken bodies, shattered glass, and chaos. The sound kept coming, though, as car after car smashed against another. My partner and I were looking at bloody bedlam on Century Boulevard in South-Central L.A.

As usual, due to the extreme crime in that area, there were no other officers available. People were wandering around in shock, horribly injured. John and I ran from person to person, applying tourniquets, and frantically calling for ambulances and other officers.

A crowd began to form, and a man took the lead, shouting and gesturing. People gathered around him as he screamed and cursed at us because there were no ambulances and no other units responding. He turned to the usual racist rants, demanding to know why the police weren't doing more to help. John and I were covered in the blood of the suffering and the dying, trying not to be distracted by the growing crowd. The leader's words and anger, coupled with the misery and blood, was getting the crowd worked up and we knew we had a serious problem. Even as the two of us scrambled to save lives, no one else helped and the leader was on the verge of inciting a riot.

This was just prior to the Rodney King incident, and tensions in L.A. were high. The LAPD had a reputation for being aggressive, with a shoot-first-and-ask-questions-later mentality (sometimes literally). Our reputation was well earned, and the crowd was waiting for us to turn on them in violence. If we didn't do something immediately, the mob would get out of control. The problem was, not a second could be spared to diffuse the growing riot. People could bleed to death in the time we took to address the crowd.

I hurried over to the leader, who recoiled as he waited for me to attack him or draw my gun. The crowd tensed, waiting for violence. Instead I said, "Can I ask you for a favor?"

He looked back at me suspiciously, caught off-guard.

"Look," I said, "you obviously lead this group. The people respect you and want to follow you. We have people wandering around in shock, and we need to get them to lie on their backs and get their feet raised so the blood will go into their brains—or they could die. Can you mobilize everyone and get that done? This way, my partner and I can stop the bleeding until we can get some ambulances here."

Once I acknowledged him as an equal and affirmed his status as a leader, the man went into immediate action, organizing people and helping us. He stood on one of the cars shouting orders. Within a minute, we had fifty people looking after the wounded. The chaos was replaced instantly by a sense of community as we all worked together to save lives.

In a moment of chaos, a true leader stepped forward and coordinated others toward a solution. You can see he was a Victor who responded in frustration until space was cleared for him to declare revolution. In that moment, he shed his resentment of the LAPD and led people. An interdependent community formed with a focused solution to an awful problem. A gang of people ready to devolve into violence was turned into a team sacrificing personal fulfillment for the good of the whole.

Tough Choices

Victors can easily be identified as people with a relentless pursuit to deliver satisfaction in their relationships. They understand that this can only be done with an unwavering dedication to interdependence, character, and truth. Without these, success will always be temporary, because there is no foundation to respond to the ever-changing needs and demands of their relationships.

When you look at successful businesses, you can see organizations where personnel decisions are made swiftly and decisively.

Many people think it's cruel to fire unproductive people. That's a strange idea. A leader's job is to have the best team, division, or company that he or she can. If a leader tolerates incompetence, that leader is not doing the job well.

Wouldn't it seem odd if a football coach didn't play the best players? Does anyone think it's cruel for an NFL coach to cut a player when he finds a better one to fill that spot? A friend of mine played in the NFL and told me how he was cut from a team the day after he was named special teams player of the game. He was a backup tight end, and the team had a starting linebacker go down with an injury. They wanted to keep the hurt player on the roster but needed another linebacker for a few weeks until the starter healed. In order to make room, they cut my friend.

Someone said they thought it was unfair considering how great my friend played the day before. "But what did his accomplishments from the day before have to do with the needs of the team for the next week?" I asked. He still thought it was unfair so I asked the tough question, "Why should that team not do what it needs to do to win just so my friend can have a job? If he had been the starting tight end, he wouldn't have been cut."

Interesting that most people would not argue about cutting an unproductive player in favor of a better player in the game of football, but we think it's cruel in the game of life. Victors say it's unfair to allow a mediocre person to keep a job rather than make room for a more talented person to have an opportunity. The upshot of this is that with Victors leading, everyone must strive to be their best in order to keep their jobs, thereby elevating the collective talent pool of the entire organization.

Optimism that Inspires

False optimism is the opiate of Victims. Victims tell stories about how great things are going to be, ignoring truth and manipulating facts. They appease the masses because their real goal is not growth, but control. Victors declare that things aren't necessarily great; circumstances are what they are, and the leader will organize to meet the challenges.

When the Marine General Chesty Puller was leading in the Korean War, an Army colonel retreated into his camp. He pulled General Puller aside and told him they were surrounded by the enemy. The colonel wanted to know what they should tell the men so they didn't get disillusioned.

General Puller walked out to his Marines and said, "Men, I want you to know that we are completely surrounded by the enemy. Now you can fire in any direction and hit them!"

General Puller didn't offer nonsense or smokescreens about how great everything was. He spoke the truth and allowed people to deal with things as they really were, instead of how he wished they were.

Passion and Discipline

Victors demonstrate both passion and discipline. Listen to some people's conversations and you can hear them often use one of the words without the other. Each is needed to be successful. If a person has one without the other:

Discipline without passion = contempt for others
Passion without discipline = contempt from others

In a major crime or disaster scene, the Los Angeles Police Department sets up a command post from which the situation can be observed and orders given. An LAPD captain told me once that when he walked into a command post, if he had to ask who was in charge, then no one was. In other words, in a crisis, Victors are obvious through their presence. This is because they exhibit a plethora of both passion and discipline.

Disciplined people who lack passion are filled with contempt for others and project arrogance. Passionate people without discipline are scattered, attracting contempt from others. This does not mean both must be present in equal portions, but both must be present.

This leads to another characteristic of Victors: Victors strive to be "right" rather than "not wrong." You've heard the sports cliché, "We play to win!" Great teams play to win, staying aggressive even when they're ahead. Mediocre teams play not to lose, getting ultraconservative when they get a lead, often losing because of their safe, predictable approach. There is a huge difference in *playing to win* versus *playing not to lose*. The first is done with discipline and passion; the second is done in insecurity and fear.

Life is 10 percent what happens to you and
ninety percent how you respond to it.
Lou Holtz

In the game of life, though, a disease has taken over Western society. The Victims have declared that we must no longer play life to be right; we must play it to not be wrong. Being right requires passion and discipline; it requires truth and conviction. Abraham Lincoln was right and millions were granted their freedom, despite the cost to him personally. Lincoln made the choice to experience great pain rather than the continued suffering of a society built on the denial of basic human rights to some groups of people.

One can be successful only by playing life to be right, not by playing not to be wrong. The world needs a good dose of Victors declaring what is and has always been so, in order to form effective solutions to real problems. Only when the basic foundation of truth has been declared can we move on to shaping the future. It is important to note that few great people are loved in their time and place. They are loved later, when the results of their relentless pursuit of truth has come to fruition.

The Need for Interdependence

We need to form interdependent communities in order to overcome the growing numbers and aggressiveness of the Victims. What is an interdependent community? In fact, the world has nearly always been formed on these, and it is only recently that we've lost touch with them. In small-town America, everyone had a contribution to make to society. Anyone refusing to contribute was excluded from the community. People worked together to form a cohesive unit. The farmer, blacksmith, handyman, clergy, doctor, and school-teacher all worked together, acknowledging their unique roles and often bartering skills. Everyone understood and needed each other's contributions.

Even large cities broke into small communities. Services all needed to be within walking distance. The policemen walked foot beats, lighting the gas streetlights at night, and greeted everyone by name. The advance in technology has produced communities where people move past one another, never having to form relationships. Where we are ignorant of one another, fear can take hold. We don't know our police officers and they don't know us as they speed by in their cars.

This is what is empowering the cynical leaders of today. They are tapping into the resentment of the American people who have for too long been told they are victims. They are being empowered by forming mobs through empty promises of entitlement and recognition.

If you are taught bitterness and anger, then you will believe you are a victim. You will feel aggrieved and the twin brother of aggrievement is entitlement. So now you think you are owed something and you don't have to work for it and now you're on a really bad road to nowhere because there are people who will play to that sense of victimhood, aggrievement and entitlement, and you won't have a job.

Dr. Condoleeza Rice

This process can be used for either positive or negative effects. Currently, Victims are empowered because there are fewer Victors stepping into leadership positions as too many Victors are lost in resignation and rage. Victors must not react with rage, but understand that people simply need to be shown the way while leaders create space for them to perform. Currently, the people of America believe that the ironic cynics (Victims) are the only ones with the answers. At least through the empty promises of entitlements they feel acknowledged and empowered, even if they know it is a false security. Until Victors show the way, there will be no growth but only continued degeneration into chaos.

So we've seen that Victors provide choices in life and the space to make those choices, while Victims look to take away choice and control people. Being a Victor takes dedication to truth, character, and freedom, and involves the risk that some people will reject your offer. But by making an offer and then allowing others to choose, the relationships we form are based on mutual contribution and reciprocal recognition of each other, leading to strong, interdependent relationships. The next section deals with the specifics of who we are and how we can grow as Victors.

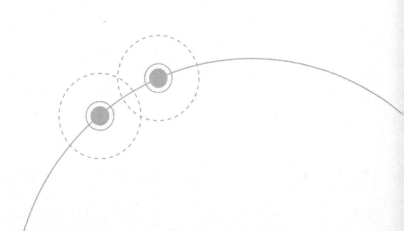

PART TWO

STRIVING FOR SOLUTIONS: EMPOWERING VICTOR ATTITUDES AND ACTIONS

8

MAKING "MARKET FORCE" WORK FOR YOU

Mastery is the capacity to observe outside the self
so that one can see what has always been so.

John Cundiff

Each person's desire is to be able to contribute to a community without being exploited. This is true in any relationship context, whether family, workplace, church, school, and even politics. When we believe we aren't being listened to or appreciated for our contribution, we experience anxiety and fall into distrust and resentment.

In order for people to contribute without feeling exploited, they must have trust in their community. Trust is often discussed, demanded, or assigned, yet is rarely defined. In order to have trust, both competence and sincerity must be present. To illustrate, John Cundiff tells the story of his teenage son wanting to go to a party with some older boys. John said no.

"Don't you trust me?" his son asked.

"I believe in your sincerity to stay out of trouble, son," John replied. "But I don't believe in your competence to stay out of trouble."

We get into trouble in our relationships because when we demand or assign trust, we are often having different conversations than other people. One person is talking about competence, while another is talking about sincerity. Both must be present to have trust.

It is important to note that trust does not produce accountability; accountability produces trust. Too often the attitude is, "Once I learn to trust you, then I'll be accountable." Of course, trust is relative. Without accountability, one can always declare trust doesn't exist, and exit when the relationship gets hard.

When I was leading a global company, I visited our Sydney office and mentioned that our San Diego office had organized a big event for clients, and of the 150 people who had RSVP'd, thirty-five didn't come. Our Sydney staff members couldn't process what I meant—it took five minutes to explain that someone would RSVP to an event and then not attend. It was almost beyond the comprehension of the Australians that someone would renege after committing to something. They acted like it was a crime. I asked what they would do about it, and they all announced that our company would never do business with them again and those clients would be ostracized from any relationships. They were all in passionate agreement. The acceptable lack of accountability in San Diego was not acceptable in Sydney.

The social tools needed to build successful relationships in today's world require a shift from trust to accountability. Trust requires a long time to build, and modern communities no longer have patience for it. Successful organizations demand accountability to have assurance promises will be kept.

Shifting from trust to accountability requires that you give up your concern for others' potential failure and replace it with your own commitment to personal responsibility—regardless of the situations and circumstances that will surely arise against you. You must have belief in a future that is not provable. This is the overwhelming risk that has weak people hide behind a lack of trust in others to justify not sailing over the horizon. People with ambition realize that the only risk is in not trading today's security for tomorrow's freedom based on personal accountability.

When someone sees accountability—when they see that even in the difficult periods of a transaction you are still committed to them—true trust is born. It's a trust that transforms the transaction into a genuine relationship.

Core Concern

Remember that in order to have trust, you need to have both sincerity and competence. Core concern is the place from which people listen. Because their core concerns are based on only one element of trust, people can hear different things from the same words:

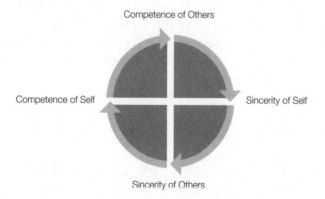

Competence of Others

Competence of Self

Sincerity of Self

Sincerity of Others

When some people wish to give or gain trust, they communicate and listen for other's competence. If you are speaking to this type of person, you must communicate that you are competent before you can move the conversation further. Some people, alternatively, are intent on communicating their own sincerity. If you want to move the trust conversation along, you must be willing to acknowledge that they are sincere.

Another group of people are focused on others' sincerity. When establishing trust with them, you must convey your genuine sincerity. The fourth group is intent on communicating their own competence, and they need to have their competence to perform acknowledged.

Notice, then, that breakdowns come often when we project our own concern onto a person who has a different core concern. If a person is trying to establish trust by communicating sincerity, they will fail if that person is listening for competence. In a job interview, a person can run through their resumé, establishing their competence, and think they did a great job. If the interviewer's core concern is competence of others, they may have. If the interviewer was listening for sincerity, they haven't.

You've probably heard the quote, "People don't care what you know until they know that you care." That is true of only some people. For the other half of the crowd, the correct quote is, "People don't care that you care until they know that you know." How we communicate is very important depending on whom we are talking to.

Elements of Style

Your core concern affects the ways you listen and communicate. It forms the foundation for how you see your interactions with others. This foundation forms a commonality in how you think and behave in transactions, which we call your style.

The following chart illustrates the style that corresponds with the previous chart. "Control" is the style that listens for other people's competence. "Influence" listens for their own sincerity to be acknowledged. "Power" listens for others' sincerity. "Authority" listens for their own competence.

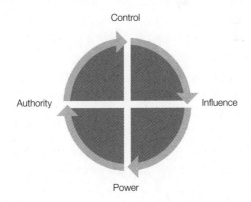

When you understand your style, you understand where you naturally fit in a transaction and how you can contribute in relationships. You become aware of your natural faults and failure points. People who understand their style are able to naturally form their identity and therefore know where they fit into relationships. People who do not understand their style spend much of their lives in confusion, unsure of where they fit into a team (be it marriage, family, work, or social network) or their place in a transaction.

When you understand other people's styles, you understand not only where you fit into a team, but where other people do as well. The exasperation of trying to communicate with people who "just don't get it" or "care only about their own agenda" fades away into obvious patterns based on their listening for their core concerns and their need to have trust acknowledged in their own way.

Once you see these obvious styles, cooperating in mutually rewarding transactions becomes simple. You become aware that each style has its own natural skills and faults, which must be developed or overcome. Therefore, each style has its own place in a community or in a transaction. When we learn to work within this clear pattern of who we are and who others are, we're able to form effective partnerships and teams, and develop what we call "Market Force" within the communities in which we're involved, be they family, business, or organizations.

All communities have cycles where the skills of certain styles are needed at specific times. Therefore, Market Force is dynamic. It is constantly gained or lost. When you are in the proper position in the cycle, you accelerate the transaction or relationship and gain Market Force. When you fail to contribute in the transaction or relationship, you lose Market Force. To understand your position, you must be familiar with your natural, inherent style.

It is important to note that these are not personality types, though the styles are sometimes expressed in certain personality traits. These are foundational ways of perceiving, behaving, and acting in transactions and relationships. They are more obvious in some people than others but will always be expressed strongly in moments of chaos. Let's look at the four styles:

Control: the Director

People of this style listen for other people's competence. They are often characterized as being independent or strong-willed. They are decisive and expect direct answers from those around them. They are goal-oriented, usually conveying a clear idea of what they want to accomplish before they begin working. They may become critical of others when things don't go their way. They are visionaries who are creative and bring new ideas to their teams. They work well in isolation, although they can fall into a mode of procrastination without an impending deadline.

People of this style want immediate results and may seem insensitive to the feelings of others. They are good at advising self-improvement, but if not careful, this skill can deteriorate into micro-management and demoralizing criticism. People of this style often find it difficult to share leadership and can be argumentative when others do not see things their way. They accept challenges and prefer things to be accomplished at a fast pace. When they are at their best, they are considerate and generous, using their strength to improve the lives of others. These are thinking people, who seek competence in themselves and others. These are people who need a driving purpose in their life.

Controls are fiercely determined to make things happen and may sacrifice relationships if they conflict with implementing their ideas. Controls can be seen as arrogant due to their bluntness and drive. They understand marketing and how to create the image they want.

Controls seek to mentor people. They love to impart their wisdom and creative ideas to help others. They generally enjoy challenges and work at a fast pace. Controls easily see the big picture and assume others do as well. Therefore, they often don't adequately communicate what they see and accuse others of being "stupid" for not seeing what is obvious to them.

These people are driven to make a legacy. They are constantly absorbing and processing, making them adept at sizing up situations. Controls thrive when they can generate possibilities and deliver ideas. They value knowledge and big-picture concepts but are not naturally good with details. They are good at initiating projects but not good at implementation. When presented with a problem, they're good at processing the entire situation and deciding on a solution.

Controls naturally strive for leadership. They are assertive, innovative, long-range thinkers with a natural ability to translate ideas into action. Because Controls are not naturally sensitive to people's feelings, they can be offensive without intending to, thinking they are simply stating reality. Controls often have difficulty seeing things from outside their own perspective.

Communication style: Controls generally have a direct, blunt style, preferring to "tell it like it is." Their primary focus is the bottom line, communicating with purpose and preferring to skip idle "chitchat." Controls tend to be logical and debate with facts and logic, and are uncomfortable conversing with people who "get off track." Controls typically have good talking skills and poor listening skills. They are good at telling people what to do and not good at being told what to do. Though Controls tend to be critical of others, they do not take criticism well. They have a remarkable skill at cutting through the noise in a transaction to get to the point of the matter. Because they are often tone-deaf to mood, they can be perceived as forceful, intimidating, and overbearing, causing the truth of their message to be lost to people who are offended by their bluntness.

Time frame: The future. Controls live five years out. They have the ability to see what will happen that others just can't see. Controls need to have a reason to live. They are rarely content in the moment unless they believe what they are doing is making a difference for the future. For this reason, life can sometimes pass them by. On the other hand, they can have great influence on society because of their natural drive to make an impact on the future.

How to talk to them: Be clear, specific, and brief, but do not oversimplify. Present possibilities in a logical fashion, with an overview of the relevant facts, then move to potential solutions. Focus on the anticipated results for the future. Keep the pace fast and decisive, geared toward long-term objectives. Avoid wasting their time with "touchy-feely" conversations or behaviors that could block the path to results. Do not review the past.

Confrontation: Controls are naturally confrontational. In fact, some actually relish a good fight. Since they see the world in black and white, they level criticism in the same way. They state the facts and are often surprised when people get their feelings hurt. In their minds, they are simply saying what is; if it offends you, change. Controls can lack tact, opting instead to get straight to the results and their assessments. Controls can level withering criticism and an hour later act like nothing happened. This is because to them, nothing did happen. They stated the facts and moved on but they are often clueless as to the emotional wounds their words and actions can leave on others.

Teams: Controls get along with others so long as their ideas are valued. Controls have a hard time teaming with other Controls unless there is a clear hierarchy based on competence. Controls also tend to chafe at Authority because they believe they slow them down, and at Influence because they see them as reckless and disorganized. Controls are naturally attracted to Power because they see Powers as people who will make their ideas happen.

Theme: "Notice my accomplishments. I measure my worth by results and my track record."

Natural professions: Orchestrator, surgeon, strategist, conductor, director, architect, CEO, and consultant.

Descriptives: Cavalier, logical, focused, driven, purposeful, decisive, commanding, willful, self-controlled, independent, dominant, blunt, aggressive, businesslike, structured, inventive, conceptual, ingenious, and principled.

Most important:	The idea
Time frame:	Future
Learn by:	Thinking
Promises:	Yes=maybe; No=no
Overriding concern:	Certainty
Focus:	Other's competence
Sign on desk:	"Do it now!"
Pet peeve:	Stupid people
Virtue:	Wisdom

Weaknesses:

- Confuse ideas with accomplishment
- Would rather be right than have things work
- Project arrogance in a breakdown
- Can go crazy if they suspect others know they don't know something
- Assume others see what they do, so they fail to adequately communicate

Strengths:

- Naturally focus on marketing and direction
- Others rely on Controls to see the big picture
- People count on Controls to anticipate and provide insights about the future

- Naturally decisive in a crisis
- See through the confusion of the present in order to make decisions about the future

Statements:
- "Because I said so."
- "Isn't it obvious?"
- "Get to the point."
- "It's my way or the highway."
- "To infinity and beyond!"
- "Fire!"

Control Political Leaders: Thomas Jefferson, Franklin Roosevelt, Ben Franklin, Margaret Thatcher, Josef Stalin, Newt Gingrich, Moses, Douglas MacArthur, Calvin Coolidge, Woodrow Wilson, Hillary Clinton

Control Entertainers: Madonna, Jerry Seinfeld, Bono, John Lennon, Martha Stewart, Rush Limbaugh, Lady Gaga, Bill O'Reilly, Angelina Jolie, Alec Baldwin, John Stewart, Keith Olbermann

Control Sports Figures: Michael Jordan, Bill Parcells, Bill Walsh, Barry Bonds, John Wooden, Lance Armstrong, Charles Barkley, Peyton Manning, Muhammad Ali, Alex Rodriguez

Control Business Leaders: Jack Welch, Steve Jobs, Frank Lloyd Wright, Oprah Winfrey, Bill Gates, Meg Whitman, Jerry Jones, Thomas Edison

Influence: The Facilitator

Influences develop trust around having their sincerity acknowledged. These people are enthusiastic, talkative, and stimulating. They are empathic and sensitive, often putting the needs of others above their own. They usually have a positive attitude toward people and are outgoing, persuasive, and friendly. Most people find them easy to get to know and to be around. They are good at multi-tasking, operate on intuition, and flourish in a flexible environment.

They will, however, sometimes cut corners in order to stay ahead of others. People of this style can be undisciplined with their time and often find it hard to follow through on commitments. If overextended, they may deteriorate into endless chatter and become a distraction, scattering their energy and leaving many projects unfinished. They love a good challenge and are competitive and not deterred by high-risk situations. Influences like to get a reaction from people and often use exaggeration to tell stories. They like getting recognition and are attracted to success and positions of prestige. At their best, they are able to shape the environment and negotiate differences in a way that produces momentum. These are perceptive people, who must be free to act.

They find joy in being impulsive and acting upon the idea of the moment. Influences like drawing attention to themselves. They are often the first to get a tattoo, have a Mohawk, or wear loud clothes. Influences often don't seem to care about what others think due to their obnoxious clothes or behavior, when in fact the opposite is true, they crave attention and acknowledgment.

Influences are sensitive to mood. They are cognizant of how people are feeling and responding in situations. Influences often appear to be rebels and free spirits, but they can be highly sensitive and empathetic. They are sincere people who take pride in having a wide array of friends and acquaintances. They enjoy socializing but can be loners in some circumstances. Generally, though, their primary concern is other people.

These people thrive on action and are usually fearless. Influences are fiercely independent and will not follow rules for the sake of mindless obedience. They tend to see laws and rules as suggestions, rather than absolutes. Influences can become easily bored because of their need for action and adventure.

Influences generally respond to whatever is immediately in front of them so they can often seem scattered. They are uncomfortable sitting in an office or boardroom all day and tend to be informal. Influences are optimistic, loyal when their freedom is not at stake, and generous.

Influences are often committed to their own belief in what's right and what's wrong, which may or may not coincide with the rules in place. The established rules have little value to Influence, unless they coincide with their own convictions. They typically make things up as they go along, rather than following a plan.

Influences love to be the center of attention and entertain people to make them happy. They want life to be a continual party; they love people, and everybody loves them. They genuinely like most people and are perplexed if others don't like them. Influences love life and like to bring others along for the ride.

Communication style: They like to talk. They may talk too much, too long and consequently "oversell" or stray off the topic. They talk about ideas and feelings, and many times generalize the facts. They listen for the sake of relationship and may not remember details. They quickly develop communication openness with others. They communicate for the sake of momentum, and use their verbal skills to win people over.

Time frame: The present. Influences live completely in the moment. They can be extremely daring because the consequences of their actions simply don't occur to them. They are often the people who climb rocks or jump off bridges into rivers while others are terrified, because the possibility of death or injury just doesn't exist for them. Influence can be completely open with their emotions, whether in celebration or sorrow because they are so present in the moment. They can be the life of the party, but can also be destructive. Influences can often be addicts because they do what feels good now, without regard for tomorrow. This same trait allows them to be heroes.

How to talk to them: Plan time to communicate, preferably in a causal environment. Be friendly, ask questions, stay on topic, be open, express feelings, and have fun. Keep the pace fast, spontaneous, and stimulating. Avoid telling them what to do and never assign them boring or repetitive tasks.

You can't recruit Influences; you must challenge them. They don't respond to conversations about money; they respond to conversations about relationship. They value recognition and loyalty. Influences like to have results posted with competitive rewards. Even if the reward is small, or even just a plaque, they respond to winning and acknowledgment.

Confrontation: Influences can be confrontational. They don't seek it, the way Controls can, but they can be defensive of others on their team. They can be vocal in the criticism of processes and the inner workings of the team (be it business, family, sports), especially when they feel their freedom is being compromised. However, they reserve the right of criticism for themselves. Often, when someone else joins in with their negative assessments of a team member, Influence will attack that person because they feel he/she hasn't earned the right to be negative of their team. Their attitude about criticism of a teammate can be, "He may be a jerk, but he's my jerk."

Teams: Influence is often attracted to Authority because they see the need for the caution and organization Authority brings. As long as they don't feel their freedom jeopardized by Authority, they value the feeling of safety they bring. Influence can be repulsed by Controls who tell them what to do, but they do seek out Controls who exude confidence and certainty about the future. Influences are usually perceptive toward mood in relationships and migrate toward freedom if they don't feel valued in a group. They often repel Powers, who see them as threats to structure, so Influence can be reactionary and confrontational to Power. They can exaggerate their freedom to Power and cause unnecessary friction in order to stake a claim to their individuality.

Theme: "Notice me. I measure my worth by acknowledgment, recognition, and applause."

Natural professions: Envoy, ambassador, spy, salesperson, adventure guide, military Special Forces, rock star, and company president.

Descriptives: Adaptable, upbeat, attractive, charming, energetic, interpersonal, perceptive, provocative, curious, innovative, spontaneous, impulsive, scattered, friendly, open-minded, personal, playful, opportunistic, competitive, daring, fun, and active.

Most important:	Relationships
Time frame:	Present
Learn by:	Talking/expressing themselves
Promises:	Yes = maybe; No = maybe
Overriding concern:	Freedom
Focus:	Their own sincerity
Sign on desk:	"Why Not?!"
Pet peeve:	Slow drivers
Virtue:	Valor

Weaknesses:
- Confuse forming relationships with accomplishment
- Would rather be free than have things work
- Project impatience in a breakdown
- Can go crazy if they feel like they have to obey strict rules

Strengths:
- Naturally focus on sales
- Naturally empathetic; they sense people's moods
- Others are inspired by their boldness

Statements:
- "Do you dare me to?"
- "Give me liberty or give me death!"
- "I climbed the mountain because it was there."
- "You only live once!"
- "No one ever died wishing they spent more time at the office."
- "Ready, Fire. Aim!"

Influence Political Leaders: George Washington, John Kennedy, Nancy Pelosi, Adolf Hitler, Winston Churchill, Alexander the Great, Theodore Roosevelt, King David, George W. Bush

Influence Entertainers: Tom Cruise, Jimi Hendrix, Jim Carrey, Jane Fonda, Robert Duvall, Dennis Miller, Mel Gibson, Keith Richards, James Dean, Ernest Hemingway, Lucille Ball, Ringo Starr

Influence Sports Figures: Magic Johnson, Joe Montana, Dennis Rodman, Terry Bradshaw, Clay Matthews, Aaron Rodgers, Jared Allen

Influence Business Leaders: Richard Branson, Mark Cuban

Power: The Builder

Powers build trust by listening for other people's sincerity. People of this style are characterized as diligent, agreeable, and dependable. They enjoy implementing structures to create stability and consistency for everyone involved. They thrive on managing many projects at the same time, because having a heavy workload makes life meaningful. People of this style have a hard time saying no to requests for favors, which can cause them to be overworked and stressed.

They may have difficulty prioritizing their numerous tasks, which can lead to them having more work than they can realistically do, causing them to express frustration. They work naturally in teams, always making sure everyone is included in the process. As a result, they have an excellent ability to create alliances and gain support from others. While they dislike personal conflict, if they perceive that their stability is threatened, they may begin to gossip or blame others for project failures.

People of this style approach risk cautiously and are resistant to change. Trust and loyalty are very important to them. At their best, they are sympathetic, dependable and generous and help to build interpersonal team connections. These are industrious people who produce great amounts of tangible value and seek to be accepted by all.

Powers like people and are driven to make sure everyone is included. Their favorite words are fairness and justice. They tend to be affable and look out for those around them. Because of this, Powers are good at forming longstanding relationships.

These people get their identity from belonging to groups and like to belong to exclusive groups and clubs. The Marine Corps is a perfect example of a Power organization. They pride themselves on being best in the military. Powers will readily wear the badge of the special groups to which they belong.

Powers like the status of belonging and take pride and identity in the groups of which they're a part. Powers truly believe the motto, "You can judge a man by his friends." In others words, one's identity comes from who he or she associates with and what groups they belong to. Powers can turn especially hostile when they are fired or kicked out of a group, because they feel their identity is being taken away.

Powers feel a strong sense of responsibility and duty. They take their responsibilities very seriously and can be counted on to follow through. Because they intensely dislike conflict, Powers do not usually express their difficulties verbally. Therefore, they are often taken advantage of and can be overly critical of themselves.

In contrast to Influence, Powers like laws and clear lines of authority. They want things to be done in familiar ways. They value tradition, fairness, security and kindness. They can blindly accept rules without questioning them in order to fill their need for security. They are clear about the way things should be and believe that existing systems are there because they work. A negative to this is that Powers can sometimes tolerate injustice in order to avoid upsetting their need for stability.

Powers can be underappreciated because they refuse to demand acknowledgment for their work. They often believe that, though they deserve more credit than they're getting, it's wrong to demand a reward for doing work, which they see as a virtue.

Communication style: Their speaking is less direct and it may take them time to develop an open form of communication. They may not speak their feelings openly, choosing instead to show them in action (e.g., by slamming a door). They actively listen to others, and they enjoy using their verbal skills to promote unity and consensus, though they may say what others want to hear in order to be accepted. Powers make better listeners than talkers.

Time frame: Three months out. Powers love work, but they are truly the opposite of Control in that they do not see the big picture. They work diligently and relentlessly on their project, looking around only long enough to make sure they're still working with the team and then getting back to work. They are the builders that get things done, but they can work themselves completely off track. They generally don't see the long-term future beyond their current project.

How to talk to them: Focus on the nuts and the bolts, and demonstrate that they will be included in the process. Present new ideas gently and provide them with guarantees and time to "let the seed grow." Be agreeable and sincere. Concentrate on the specifics of "how" things will get done, and draw out their suggestions and opinions. Ask them what is on their list and then don't interrupt until they're done. Keep the pace casual and personal, yet remain focused on the production goals. Avoid pushy, aggressive behavior and don't disrupt their work with conceptual conversations about the future.

Confrontation: Powers don't handle confrontation well. If being attacked or criticized, they tend to become quiet and often will not defend themselves, but they'll curse under their breath. If they need to confront, they will tend to drop hints or leave small clues, hoping the team will figure out the issue. They are active listeners, listening for meaning in things that are not said and watching body language. Powers can be passive-aggressive and petty rather than confrontational, subverting the process for the sake of revenge. When dealing with Power, it is important to listen or watch for their clues of when they are uncomfortable, because they will usually not say anything.

Teams: Powers are the only style that truly like all of the styles. They get along well with each other and with everyone else, as long as people are getting the project done. In fact, if people aren't contributing, Power will often simply move them out of the way and do both jobs rather than have to stop the process to deal with the issue. Powers are naturally attracted to Control because they like Control's ability to see the big picture and dictate projects. If Power has confidence in a Control, they can be fiercely loyal. Powers can sometimes become irritated with Influence when they believe Influence's need for freedom and independence threatens the productivity of the team. They can become irritated with Authority when they believe that their rules and structure inhibit Power's ability to get work done. In either case though, Power will usually just try to work around the issue, rather than confront it.

Theme: "Notice my abilities and effort. I measure my worth by how much attention I get from others."

Natural professions: General, office manager, law enforcement officer, judge, schoolteacher, chief operating officer, union member, career military people, nurse, caregiver.

Descriptives: Engaging, likeable, responsible, amenable, supportive, inclusive, accepting, considerate, amiable, reliable, steady, feeling, loyal, pleasant, compatible, consistent, harmonious, compassionate, devoted, sympathetic, and fair.

Most important:	Be part of a team
Time frame:	Ninety days
Learn by:	Listening
Promises:	Yes=yes; No=no
Overriding concern:	Stability
Focus:	Others; sincerity
Sign on desk:	"My office is your office"
Pet peeve:	Rude people
Virtue:	Justice

Weaknesses:
- Confuse activity for progress
- Project frustration in a breakdown
- Can go crazy if they are excluded from the group

Strengths:
- Naturally focus on getting things done—production
- Create alliances
- People count on Power to bring structure
- Bring fairness and peace to a group

Statements:
- "You can judge a man by his friends."
- "Let's get buy-in from everyone."
- "The few, the proud, the Marines."
- "To do or die, not to reason why."
- "The devil you know is better than the devil you don't know."
- "Ready. Aim. Fire"

Power Political Leaders: Ronald Reagan, Bill Clinton, General Schwarzkopf, King Saul, General Robert E. Lee, Ted Kennedy

Power Entertainers: Sally Field, Paul McCartney, George Clooney, Regis Philbin, Jennifer Aniston, Mark Wahlberg, Johnny Carson

Power Sports Figures: Howie Long, Bo Jackson, Larry Bird, Derek Jeter, Mark McGuire, Tim Tebow

Power Business Leaders: Donald Trump, Mitt Romney

Authority: The Analyzer

People of this style are typically the rational, orderly type, ultimately concerned with maintaining high quality and standards. They dislike waste and sloppiness, and are often characterized as conscientious, disciplined, and serious. They like things to be logical, organized, and to comply with any preexisting rules. People of this style are persistent when seeking clarification, often asking very specific questions about the minutest of details so they understand every angle of what someone is trying to do. They are deliberate and cautious before taking action, and many times work backward to reach their decisions by using a process of elimination.

Most prefer to work by themselves in an objective, task-oriented, intellectual environment. They may be hypersensitive to criticism and can deteriorate into moodiness or counterattacks when they believe others perceive them as incompetent, unprepared, or disorganized. At their best, they are discerning and rigorous, often calling a group back to its root values. These are exacting, judging individuals who thrive on their work life. They demand professionalism, organization, and efficiency.

Authorities wake up in the morning looking for a dilemma. This can make them effective team members as a healthy Authority naturally looks for problems to solve. With Authority on the team, loose ends get taken care of. Sloppiness is not tolerated and incompetence gets stamped out. Authorities are more concerned with quality and efficiency than popularity. They are very difficult to throw off-track when they decide to solve a problem.

These people study everything and everyone around them. They don't originate new ideas but they make other people's ideas better. For this reason, Authorities have a hard time making decisions. They can analyze a problem to death and therefore have difficulty making choices. Most great actors are Authorities because of their uncanny ability to observe the nuances of the people and things around them.

An example of Authority in Market Force can be seen in the mission to the moon. The rocket was off course 99 percent of the time, thus scientists were constantly monitoring and adjusting the flight pattern to get the exact coordinates needed in each moment to accomplish the goal of the mission. Authority acts like this in a healthy transaction. Control declares the future, Influence creates the momentum, Power does the work, but Authority keeps the process on-line. Without Authority, the process quickly spins out of control and people often forget what the goal was in the first place.

Authorities have a strongly felt internal sense of duty, which lends them a serious air and a dedication to quality and follow-through. They are organized and methodical and can be depended on to do the "right thing." While they generally take things seriously, they can have an offbeat sense of humor. Many comedians are Authorities because they have a knack for observing and imitating others.

These individuals respect laws and traditions, and expect the same from others. They believe that things should be done according to procedures and plans. Unhealthy Authorities can be obsessed with rules and structure, insisting on doing everything "by the book." They can become the person who thinks it is their responsibility to make sure no one else is having fun.

Authorities like to be accountable for their actions. Authorities need facts and usually have good memories for them. They may have difficulty understanding different perspectives and it is hard to convince them of a new idea or way of thinking, unless there is proof. Once Authority supports the idea, they can be tenacious in their commitment to its success.

Authorities are often out of touch with their own feelings and the feelings of others, and can be uncomfortable expressing affection and emotion. They live primarily inside their own minds, having the ability to analyze difficult problems, identify patterns, and come up with logical explanations. They strive to achieve logical conclusions to problems, and don't understand the importance or relevance of applying subjective emotional considerations to decisions.

Communication style: They keep their distance communication-wise and don't naturally mingle. Often they conceal their true feelings and ideas when first asked, preferring instead to think through an entire topic before answering. People of this style focus on the details and consistently remember them. Typically, they communicate well with the written word. Their ability to listen is stronger than their ability to speak and communicate.

Time frame: The past. Authority knows how things have been done in the past. They often have very good memories for what has occurred and what was said. They can recall the facts of past transactions and be a great resource in analyzing past successes and failures. Authority is often unable to understand the present and cannot see the future, but they can be an invaluable resource to those who do. They keep the team from repeating the mistakes of yesterday and hold others accountable to the commitments they have made.

How to talk to them: Be prepared and organized. Present details along with the pros and cons. Document everything. Give solid evidence, be serious, and allow time for questions. Do not force a decision. Listen respectfully and take notes regarding their assessments. Keep the pace systematic and formal. Avoid surprises, inconsistency and unpredictability.

Confrontation: Authority is not naturally confrontational but can become so without knowing it. They simply state facts and their assertions about the past, surprised when they offend people. Authority can become consciously and vigorously confrontational when their security is being threatened. When confronted,

Authority can argue for hours. Their usual method is to avoid uncomfortable facts by asking a relentless array of questions, meant to expose the ignorance of the person confronting them so that they don't have to deal with the point being made.

They are often more concerned with being right than they are with the truth, if the truth threatens their worldview or their security. Authorities can outlast anyone and can literally survive confrontation by exhausting those around them.

Teams: Authority naturally seeks out Influence. Friendships with Influence usually help Authority to have more fun in life while Authority helps Influence to have structure in their lives. Authorities can be offended by Control because of Control's assertions about the future without any proof. They can be bothered by Power and their constant work, because Authority often sees this as creating more messes for them to clean up. Authorities tend to respect each other but have few genuine relationships with anyone other than Influence. Authority are often the most intelligent members of the team, that is to say, they have the most facts, but they often don't know how to implement the facts into a vision for the future. They need a team so that their intellect can be implemented in a positive way.

Theme: "Notice my efficiency. My personal worth can be measured by precision, accuracy, and progress."

Natural professions: Chief financial officer, doctor, auditor, lawyer, author, actor, accountant, professor, and judge.

Descriptives: Prudent, confrontational, precise, conservative, methodical, introspective, pensive, structured, organized, perfectionist, persistent, systematic, thorough, prepared, deliberate, formal, functional, credible, accurate, procedural, traditional, and conventional.

Most Important:	Preserving what they have
Time frame:	The past
Learn by:	Reading
Promises	Yes=yes; No=maybe
Overriding concern:	Security
Focus:	Own competence
Sign on desk:	"Put it in writing!"
Pet peeve:	Inefficiency
Virtue:	Prudence

Weaknesses:

- Would rather have an impact than have things work
- Project indifference in a breakdown
- Can go crazy if they are forced to decide
- Insist others maintain their standards, whether they are productive or not

Strengths:

- Naturally focus on administration and improving processes
- Others rely on Authority to enforce standards
- Naturally review what happened and assess what went right or wrong

Statements:

- "A penny saved is a penny earned."
- "I told you so!"
- "Quality over quantity."
- "This is how it's always been done."
- "It's all about the fundamentals."
- "Ready. Aim. Aim. Aim…"

Authority Leaders: Abraham Lincoln, Condoleeza Rice, Barack Obama, Apostle Paul, John Adams, Ruth Bader Ginsberg, George H. W. Bush, James Madison, Billy Graham, Bobby Kennedy

Authority Entertainers: Clint Eastwood, Julia Roberts, Dustin Hoffman, Courtney Cox, Ted Koppel, Ray Romano, Denzel Washington, Michael Landon, George Harrison, Larry David, Tom Hanks, John Steinbeck

Authority Sports Figures: Tom Brady, Bill Walton, Tom Landry, Pat Summit, Tiger Woods, Tony Dungy, Eli Manning

Authority Business Leaders: Mark Zuckerberg, Warren Buffett, Ben Stein, Alan Greenspan, Ben Bernanke, Sam Walton

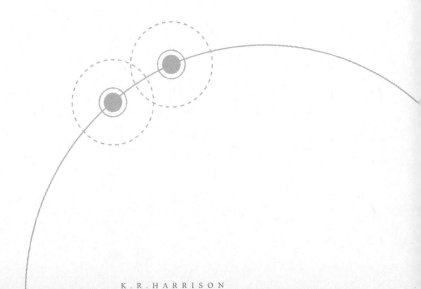

9

THE FOUR STYLES IN ACTION

Whether you think you can or think you can't, you're right.

Henry Ford

In relationships, Control and Influence pull, while Power and Authority push. You cannot attract or lead Controls by pushing them or making them feel obligated. In order to attract them, you must form a vacuum that pulls them in. Control is attracted when they see a place where their ideas can be appreciated and implemented, where they can have the freedom to think without coercion. Influence is attracted where they have the freedom to be themselves, work at their own pace and be driven by competition and acknowledgment. Both styles lead effectively in the same way.

Power and Authority are attracted by the idea of a secure, established team with a clear identity and plan. They do respond to obligation and duty; Power naturally appears where there is work to be done and there is a team to which they can belong. Authority is attracted where they see they can make things better. Both styles lead from these same foundations.

Control

Controls lead by pulling others behind them. They stand above the crowd declaring the future with little to no evidence, because they see what others can't. Controls attract people through their confidence and competence. They make bold predictions and attract people who help them make their predictions come true. Effective leaders are often viewed as larger-than-life and above the group they lead. A great example is Moses, leading the people of Israel out of Egypt and into a vast desert to found their own country. He had no plan, didn't know where he was going and was facing enemies at every turn, yet he boldly declared a future and gave assurance to millions of people, creating a nation that still exists to this day.

Effective Control example: Thomas Jefferson starts the Declaration of Independence with classic Control language, "We hold these truths to be self evident. . . ." In other words, "The truth is obvious." Jefferson lived in the future. He was the architect of the University of Virginia. He decided to proceed with the Louisiana Purchase, a bold transaction at the time that earned him significant criticism. Jefferson made the move, despite the opposition, because he saw what others couldn't—that the U.S. had the capacity to stretch across the continent, and would be much more secure and powerful if it did so.

Jefferson's battles with Hamilton were notorious, but he didn't allow himself to get sidetracked, as Control often does. He stuck with his vision. Jefferson was also able to wait on his agenda in deference to George Washington's. Jefferson was a brilliant thinker who saw a bigger picture than others and refused to be sidetracked from it.

I have found it advisable not to give too much heed
to what people say when I am trying to accomplish something
of consequence. Invariably they proclaim it can't be done.
I deem that the very best time to make the effort.

Calvin Coolidge

Effective Control example: When the British and U.S. governments were running a naval blockade and things got politically difficult for President George H. W. Bush (Authority), he called British Prime Minister Margaret Thatcher to explain. Her response? "You're not going all wobbly on me, now are you, George?"

Margaret Thatcher came to power in a different world than today. She not only didn't let her gender get in her way, she relished the difficulties it brought, shocking her opponents with her combativeness. Mrs. Thatcher had Control's ability to confront the powerful mining unions, the Irish Republican Army and even President Reagan with absolute resolve.

Ineffective Control Example: Richard Nixon. When I graduated from Marine Corps Officer Candidate School in 1986, I had the privilege of staying with a retired 3-star admiral and the top doctor in the U.S. Navy. He had been the personal physician to presidents Roosevelt, Johnson, Nixon, and Reagan. He told me that Roosevelt (Control) and Reagan (Power) both had the ability to make whomever they were speaking to feel like the most important person in the room. Both had an inherent humility; they drew people to themselves and inspired great loyalty. He contrasted them with Johnson and Nixon (ineffective Controls), who exuded arrogance and detachment. He said that Nixon felt it necessary to remind anyone he spoke to that he was the President of the United States. An ineffective Control, Nixon was paralyzed by insecurity. My friend noted that Nixon's staff did not stay loyal to him because of his actions. He pointed out that if Reagan were ever accused of a scandal, his staff would stay loyal to the end, due to his humility and Market Force leadership. A year later, Iran-Contra broke and Reagan's staff did indeed stay loyal.

The very nature of Watergate illustrates unhealthy Control. Market Force Controls understand the importance of image. They declare the future and foster an image consistent with their declaration. Poor Controls realize the importance of image as well. However, rather than persevering through the commitment and work required, they elevate themselves by pushing down others. They descend into spying, playing politics, and false accusations, building their reputation through the destruction of others, rather than elevation of purpose.

Influence

Influences lead by pulling through motivation. They inspire others through brave examples, self-sacrifice, and bold speeches. They stand in front of the crowd and are often the example of the behavior they espouse. Effective leaders are often viewed as heroes, leading through valiant action from the front of the group.

Ninety-nine percent of the failures come from people who
have the habit of making excuses.

George Washington

Effective Influence example: George Washington bucked huge
odds leading a small band of farmers and merchants against the
greatest army in the world. He often fought in battles personally and was seen leading charges at the enemy from the front.
He was a larger-than-life character who inspired a sense of awe
in those around him. Washington was not known as an intellectual, yet he garnered complete loyalty from great minds like
Benjamin Franklin, John Adams, Thomas Jefferson, and James
Madison. Washington was successful in large part because he
never got lost in the impossibility of the task. He concentrated
on winning the present and seemed unconcerned with the
doubt of the future.

At Valley Forge, Washington could have gone back to
Virginia to the warmth of his estate, something that was completely acceptable in that day. The British had retreated for
the winter and there was no reason for the commander to be
present. In typical Influence fashion, Washington sacrificed
for his men, stirring them to unrelenting dedication and unity
behind the cause.

In one of the first battles of the Revolutionary War,
Washington's men fled in panic from the advancing British.
Washington's generals watched in their usual safe place from
atop a hill in disgust as the men fled in panic. To their hor-
ror, they watched General Washington ride to the front lines,
punching fleeing soldiers and ordering them to turn and fight,
as bullets screamed by him. Washington rode into the battle,
fighting hand-to-hand with the British, disappearing in the
gun smoke.

One of his generals said he knew Washington was dead and the Revolution was over before it really got started. A few minutes later, Washington emerged from the smoke, still cutting down enemy soldiers with his sword. His men saw that he was willing to risk more than any of them had and their loyalty to him was sealed on that day. This is leadership by Influence, Washington was oblivious to the risks or the immense risks to the army if he got killed; he simply led in the moment, doing what needed to be done with great courage.

Effective Influence example: A story is told of Joe Montana in the Super Bowl against the Cincinnati Bengals. The 49ers had the ball with time running out and needed to drive the ball the length of the field to win. The team was tense as they gathered for the drive. Montana, as an Influence, naturally sensed their tense mood. As they waited during a timeout, Montana pointed to the end zone and said, "Hey look, it's John Candy!" The players looked up, shocked that he would notice something like that at such an important moment. And sure enough, John Candy sat in the other end zone. "Let's drive the ball down to John Candy," Montana said. Their mood lightened and they did it. One of the players said afterward that they all just knew Joe would do it.

This is classic Influence leadership: sense the mood, point the way, and scream, "We can do it!" Contrast this to Control who says, "This is what needs to be done, now do it!" One of the reasons Influence can inspire with such grandeur is their ability to live completely in the moment. Most of the 49er players were tense with the weight of responsibility of winning the NFL championship and the consequences of losing.

They were thinking of all the work and sweat to get where they were and it all came down to one last possession. Market Force Influence is oblivious to such a burden. They are able to shrug, point to the end zone and say, "Let's just do what we've done all year. Just drive the ball down and score. What's the big deal?"

Ineffective Influence example: Adolf Hitler accomplished incredible feats by taking over a country with rampant inflation, a terrible economy, and no military. In only seven years, he was close to conquering Europe. He inspired by speeches that restored the pride of the German people. He stirred them to such great frenzy that they blindly followed him into world war.

Hitler was brilliant at sensing the mood of the German people. They had rejected him roundly ten years earlier, but now their resentment toward the French over World War I, their horrible economy, and the growing fear of communism had them seeking bold leadership at any cost. Hitler did what all wicked leaders do— he found someone to blame the problems on, united the people against common enemies, and destroyed anyone who disagreed with him. Influences have the ability to stir passion in people, which can be used for great good or great evil.

Power

Powers lead from within the group. They push the group along through the force of their will and by actively empathizing with those they are leading. They lead by identifying with those among them and becoming an illustration of their better self. Powers are seen as one of the group who has reached their ultimate potential. They appeal to the senses of justice, fairness and community in the group to convince others to follow them.

Effective Power example: Ronald Reagan became president while Democrats dominated Congress and were opposed to Reagan's ideology. Reagan did not declare the future and instruct congress as a Control, give grand speeches or challenge them, as an Influence, or steadfastly appeal to a sense of right or wrong, as an Authority. He demonstrated classic Power leadership by taking his case to the people. He appealed to his "Fellow Americans," one of his favorite phrases, on what the country ought to do. He led from within, making it clear that he was one of the people. He declared that being an American was something special, part of an elite group. Americans rallied around Reagan and his changes became reality through the force of the people.

If you're afraid of the future, then get out of the way, stand aside. The people of this country are ready to move again.

Ronald Reagan

Effective Power example: One of the gifts of Power is to be able to change their approach, agenda and even their personality when necessary to get the job done. When Bill Clinton took office, he had a majority in both houses of Congress and attempted to use it to aggressively press his agenda. When the country rejected his ideas and gave complete congressional control to the Republicans, electing a Control in Speaker Newt Gingrich, Clinton was able to pivot his approach. Rather than live in resentment, he worked with Congress to pass several key bills, reform welfare and balance the budget. Clinton illustrates a flexible Power who was able to work against great odds to get portions of his agenda through.

This is a gift that Power brings in such circumstances. Control would be more likely to take a stand and demand their way or the highway (as Gingrich did). Authority would tend to live in denial and continue governing the same ineffective way, butting against an immovable congress. Influence would opt not to run for reelection or would become belligerent in their attitude to the job. Power has the ability to change with the mood and the times, continuing to make progress when all seems lost.

Ineffective Power example: Mitt Romney came across as a likable and kind-hearted man in his presidential contest with Barack Obama. However, he had projected a very distinctive image as the governor of Massachusetts (liberal Republican), another in business (decisive business leader), another in the Republican primaries (conservative Republican) and yet another in the election campaign. He had effectively morphed his brand for his audience as he needed—as Powers so effectively do.

In the end, though, he was unable to project an effective identity; the public questioned who the real Mitt Romney was. People tend to want their politicians to fit into a box. Reagan and Clinton were also able to change their image as needed, but they led with a strong overriding personality, which Romney did not do.

Romney also displayed Power's natural resistance to confrontation. When he overcame this natural tendency in the first debate, the public responded to him and his poll numbers rose dramatically. In the third debate, though, he completely avoided conflict and refused to bring up controversial issues that surrounded the president. He stated that he chose to be "presidential." In reality, he made excuses to avoid confrontation, costing him the election.

Authority

These people lead by declaring the right thing. The effective leader steadfastly pushes from behind the group, never wavering in his or her commitment to reaching the goal. They support their cause through exhaustive information and analysis and a refusal to compromise. They convince others to follow them through an unwavering commitment to their standards.

Effective Authority example: Most people think of Abraham Lincoln as our greatest president, yet he was elected with less than 40 percent of the vote. During his presidency, he was extremely unpopular and actively mocked by the public and the press. He lost nearly every election he ran in, yet his story of perseverance is truly astounding. Lincoln never waivered in his convictions, even as the country spiraled toward civil war.

Be sure you put your feet in the right place, then stand firm.
Abraham Lincoln

Many people tried to convince Lincoln to back away from his stance on slavery, to issue a statement that would appease slave-holding states, but he refused. As Lincoln faced the fact that his beliefs would result in the imminent deaths of hundreds of thousands of people, he persevered. Outlasting everyone is the hallmark of Authority. Lincoln pushed the country with unrelenting conviction and changed the world through perseverance.

Effective Authority example: Tom Landry said, "I don't believe in team motivation. I believe in getting a team prepared." His first five seasons as coach of the Dallas Cowboys, Landry never won more than five games. He persisted, however, and became one of the most successful coaches in NFL history. His teams were notoriously well prepared and morally upstanding.

Landry was known for his formal suit and fedora hat while he stood on the sidelines, showing no emotion. After games, he had little to say. He had no time for grand speeches. His teams were prepared and expected to perform according to the fundamentals they had been taught. This is Authority in leadership: preparation, each detail accounted for, flawless execution demanded, and no excuses tolerated.

Ineffective Authority example: John Adams was also a man who was grounded in his beliefs, and he had accomplished great things in the United States. He defended the British soldiers in the Boston Massacre hearings, was a framer of the Declaration of Independence, and threw his weight behind Jefferson and

Washington at key points. However, when he was sent to Paris to raise funds for the fledgling country, he failed miserably.

Benjamin Franklin, a Control who was widely respected throughout the U.S., was already in France and had created a strong brand for himself by wearing a coonskin cap and generally playing up the American frontiersman stereotype to the French. Adams was unable to adapt to the French and was offended both by them and by Franklin. Adams' inability to be flexible endangered negotiations and Franklin wrote to Congress to have him removed. Adams was sent to The Netherlands, an Authority-dominated culture at that time, where he was successful among his own kind.

Note that in the examples of the ineffectual leaders, all were successful. However, all of them display the negative aspects of their style in glaring ways: Nixon's brashness and arrogance, Hitler's extreme passion in the moment with no regard about its effects on people . . . Romney's need for acceptance and avoidance of confrontation . . . and Adams' persistence in his opinions causing him to be deaf to his audience. One can be successful but still be deeply flawed. Be aware of the natural faults each style inherently project so you can overcome them in yourself and those around you.

Examples of Market Force in Life

Seeing the styles in people we know or in characters on the screen can be a helpful way of recognizing their respective behaviors. Characters in stories tend to have their traits concentrated and exaggerated for the sake of the story. It is truly amazing how good writers naturally pick up on the four styles. One can see them in good books and movies all the time.

Control

The movie *Gladiator* is a great example of the Control style at its best. Russell Crowe plays a general whose men are completely loyal. He is betrayed by the new emperor, a Power who is obsessed with his popularity. Forced into slavery as a gladiator, he mobilizes the men around him. Because of his command, presence and competence, they follow him and become a unified group withstanding all the hardships thrown at them. Crowe's character knows how to "market" himself, building a brand that wins over the people of Rome. The movie shows a healthy Control naturally attracting others to follow him. He is completely aware of his own identity, creating a brand that elevates him beyond his status. Crowe's character never has to state that he is a leader—others see it in him and push him to the front.

Influence

The Notebook is a love story and a good example of two Influences involved in a relationship. Rachael McAdams plays an Influence stuck in the rules of wealthy Southern society. When Ryan Gosling's character meets her, she's attracted to his freedom of spirit. She resists him at first, but he wins her over in a way Influences have a hard time resisting—he challenges her. Later in the movie, she says, "Look at us, we're fighting already."

"That's what we do, we fight," he says.

Two Influences in a relationship will have passion, with great highs and lows, and it will never be boring.

Braveheart is the ultimate Influence movie, but it also shows how the distinct styles work together, or against each other. Mel Gibson's character, William Wallace, is a man who values freedom above all else. He refuses to live under the tyranny of English rule. The Scottish nobility lives in relative comfort, security, and safety, yet Wallace chafes at English rule and defies it with every chance he gets. When his wife is killed, Wallace motivates the passive Scots through his sheer passion for freedom. Wallace's cries are for "Freedom!" and he would rather die than live in security without liberty.

Wallace uses his unwavering daring to mobilize the Scots to risk their lives. He leads from the front and is never thrown off-course by who will or will not follow him into battle. Wallace never stops to contemplate what his end game might be. He certainly doesn't have the ability to march on London, but he is a master at winning the battle in front of him and letting tomorrow deal with itself. In the end, he sacrifices himself for the cause.

The father-and-son team that become Wallace's main lieutenants are a typical portrayal of Market Force Powers. They challenge Wallace and test him before they're willing to commit. Once they are assured of his commitment to the cause, they are completely loyal and refuse to be left out of any battle or negotiation. They are offended at any suggestion that Wallace make any moves without them. They get their identity from being a part of Wallace's inner circle and they will risk anything for that honor, including their lives.

The Scottish nobles are examples of unhealthy Authorities. These men argue and accuse each other, constantly wavering in their opinions. They desperately want to be like Wallace and resent him for being the man they wish they were. Their leader, Robert the Bruce, yearns to be a part of the movement, but instead gets trapped in politics and in constant survival conversations with his father, with the other nobles, and even with Wallace. He betrays Wallace, choosing security over character.

King Edward I, known as Longshanks (due to his height and stature), represents ineffective Control. He rules England with an iron hand and destroys anyone who dares to disagree with him. He has no real reason to rule Scotland; he rules it because it's there. Unhealthy Control seeks to live up to their name—to control. Longshanks simply wants to rule over Scotland because that is his nature; he thinks the more land and people that are under him, the greater he is.

King Longshanks wants to exert his dominance over any and all that he can, even if he has no idea what to do with the control once he has it. Longshanks is willing to sacrifice anyone to advance his greatness. He considers everyone around him to be incompetent or ignorant. He makes people think they are making decisions or have some form of autonomy, but he is actually working from his own plan, negotiating with France on a completely different plan to destroy Wallace than any of his people realize.

In the end, all of the characters are consistent with their identity: the nobles betray, the Powers wait for orders to help, Longshanks exerts his control, and Wallace sacrifices all, screaming "Freedom!" with his dying breath. The last scene is Robert the Bruce as a changed man, leading the army as a Market Force Authority. The Powers, content to have found another leader with solid convictions, follow him into battle.

Power

Ocean's Eleven, like *Braveheart*, has characters that demonstrate the styles in distinctive ways. The movie is a Power movie with its themes of justice, fairness, and revenge. Clooney's character is the consummate Power, out for revenge on the villain Control named Terry Benedict, played by Andy Garcia. Clooney's character, Danny Ocean, is able to put together a specialized group for a distinctive intention: to burglarize Benedict's casino. Ocean leads from within, as one of the group. His primary reason for the heist isn't the money, it's revenge and for the sake of the group.

Brad Pitt plays an Influence, as he almost always does. His character is aloof and cool. Matt Damon plays the Authority, as he always does so well. In fact, watching just about any Matt Damon movie is a good example of Authority. Damon's character lives in constant fear of anyone thinking he isn't the expert on something.

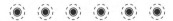

Places in the Heart is also a good Power example. Sally Field plays a widow in rural Texas who is going to lose her land to the bank. She mobilizes people to come help her and works her way through planting the field with cotton, even when everyone tells her it can't be done. Her character doesn't get distracted with "what if?" scenarios about failure. She forms a team and works with dogged determination until the job is done.

Authority

Perhaps the greatest example of Market Force Authority in a movie is *Saving Private Ryan*. Tom Hanks' character has been given orders that nearly everyone considers absurd: find one soldier, risking the lives of an entire squad. Hanks' character never questions the orders, nor does he tolerate his soldiers doing so. He is given orders and he follows them to the death, never wavering in his obedience.

Hanks' character never seeks credit and never demands loyalty. He quietly and steadily leads his men. Due to his strength of character and conviction, Hanks' men have great respect for him and are willing to risk their lives for him. The movie exemplifies how people seek absolute right and wrong, and when they think they've found it in a person or an idea, they'll risk all for it.

Gran Torino is another example of Authority. Clint Eastwood's character is a salt-of-the-earth man who has followed the rules of the American Dream. He got a good job at Ford and stayed with that company until he earned his pension. He still has every tool he ever purchased, hung in precise order on his wall. The center of the story is his Ford Gran Torino, still in pristine condition. He knows exactly how life is supposed to be lived and is deeply offended by the immigrants who have changed his neighborhood, living life differently from how he believes they should. In classic Authority fashion, Eastwood refuses to simply move, like others have. He stays in the neighborhood, persevering through intense challenges, earning the respect of his neighbors, and vise versa.

Sometimes if you want to see a change for the better,
you have to take things into your own hands.
Clint Eastwood

Actors

Looking at famous people can be a good example of styles. Think of actors who are Influences: Robert Downey, Jr., Mel Gibson, Rachael McAdams, Tom Cruise, Brad Pitt, Steve McQueen, Jane Fonda, Jim Carrey, and Robert Duvall. When you look at their roles, they almost always play Influences. Think of Robert Duvall overseeing a surf session during battle in *Apocalypse Now*, Brad Pitt's reckless need for freedom in *Legends of the Fall*, Mel Gibson in *Lethal Weapon*, Robert Downey, Jr. in *Iron Man* or *Sherlock*

Holmes. Actors who are Influences often become the ones we consider movie stars. They attract people without even being aware of it, having the ability to make people want to be like them.

Powers easily play other styles, but they tend to be attracted to Power-type stories that are centered on justice, work, and revenge. Sylvester Stallone, Liam Neeson, Charles Bronson, and others tend to star in movies that have similar story lines. Power actors, such as Sally Field, Jennifer Aniston, and George Clooney, star in movies about inclusion or overcoming all odds to succeed, like *Places in the Heart* and *Ocean's Eleven*. Powers also make great movie stars because they are adept at changing their personalities to fit their audience. They are not naturally movie stars the way Influences are—they have to work at it.

Controls have strong personalities and therefore have a difficult time fading into a character. Controls who are actors are either immensely talented, or always play a Control type of character. Angelina Jolie, Russell Crowe, Sharon Stone, Kathryn Hepburn, Sean Connery, Jimmy Stewart, and Lee Marvin are Controls. Controls dominate the screen and don't usually appear in subtle roles. Controls either project an air of intensity or of casual indifference. In the case of casual indifference, it's an act. There is always an intensity boiling underneath—some Controls have simply perfected the art of covering it.

Most truly great actors are Authorities. Authorities are not originators of ideas or behavior. Instead, they are gifted at taking other's ideas and making them better. For this reason, they become very good at imitation, able to disappear into their roles whereas the other styles often project too much of their own personality into their role.

Because they study detail, Authorities are imitators and have a knack for making things better. Authorities are adept at observing the quirks of others and doing them more distinctly, creating memorable characters. Think of a great actor and he or she is probably an Authority: Clint Eastwood, Dustin Hoffman, John Lithgow, Gary Oldman, Denzel Washington, Paul Giamatti, Julia Roberts, Tom Hanks, Paul Newman, John Voight, Gene Hackman, Leonardo DiCaprio, Jeff Bridges, Marlon Brando, and others.

Sports

Probably the best example of Market Force in sports was the Chicago Bulls of the 1990s. They were led by Michael Jordan, a Control. Jordan's intensity and dedication to winning were notorious. He had a keen eye for marketing himself and his team. Everything he did and said exemplified his image. He became a brand unto himself. Jordan was so adept at branding himself that his face and name became instantly recognizable as a part of Americana. He drove that team and only players who were dedicated to winning were invited to be a part of it. Jordan had no qualms about who the Bulls were and what they were about. The mission of the Chicago Bulls was clear and anyone who deviated from it was cut from the team.

Dennis Rodman was the Influence. He was the facilitator with an impossible mission: go out and get fifteen rebounds a game. His call to action was a challenge—take on the toughest players in the NBA, from Charles Barkley to Shaquille O'Neil, night after night, and outrebound them. That is an impossible mission, perfect for Influence.

Sometimes Rodman's commitment to being free was more important than having things work. When he lost his balance, he became more committed to his own freedom than to the intention of the team, like when he head-butted an official and was suspended for five games.

His survival conversation could be observed as, "If I have to do what other people tell me to do, I will die." This was exemplified when Coach Phil Jackson took him out of a game, and

Rodman protested on the sidelines for five minutes. When told to re-enter the game, he refused. He was action-oriented, versus thought-oriented.

Players like Rodman often don't know why they do what they do because they're not introspective. They act before they think, often letting emotion get the best of them. A Control like Jordan tolerated Rodman because his contribution was greater than the distraction of his antics.

Scottie Pippin was the Power. He was the glue that consistently held the team together. He desperately wanted to lead the team, but when Jordan retired for two years, Pippin was lost without him. Pippin seemed to wander around the court and literally resented the team for making him their leader. When Jordan returned, Pippin was able to return to his natural role and became a great player again. Pippin often complained about not getting the credit he deserved and complained about money, comparing his contract to Jordan. Pippin's concern wasn't really money—he was actually saying, "You love him more than me."

The Bulls had several Authority players and an Authority coach in Phil Jackson. The most obvious was probably Steve Kerr. He was Mr. Consistent and Mr. Fundamental. Kerr could always be counted on to hit a free throw or a three-point shot when the Bulls needed it. He was the quiet player whom people rarely noticed until he was hitting the game-winning shot.

Business

Bill Gates—Control: His foremost linguistic act is declaration, which is a promise to the future. He is always talking about the road ahead and what Microsoft will be. His operational time frame is five years out. When interviewed by Tom Brokaw, Gates spoke about his vision of the future and said that he couldn't stop working until his vision was brought into the world. At times, he appears arrogant to other people. Associates say that Gates can be aloof and overbearing. He is thought-oriented, and his major commitment is to the idea.

Richard Branson—Influence: Branson has been called a maverick by the press and a rebel by his enemies. He built his wealth through signing controversial rock bands to his fledgling record company, such as the Sex Pistols and Culture Club. Branson is a transformational leader, with his companies known for their informality. Branson champions little management structure and emphasis on autonomy. Branson said, "For me, business is not about wearing suits, or keeping stockholders pleased. It's about being true to yourself, your ideas, and focusing on the essentials." In other words, business is about freedom.

Donald Trump—Power: Listen to Trump talk for thirty seconds and you won't fail to hear him mention some famous person with whom he is a "good friend." Powers are shameless name-droppers because they seek identity from those with whom they associate. Trump exudes this. No matter how many buildings bear his name, he retains the need to trumpet his clubs, associations and friends. Trump is a tireless worker who has multiple and widely diverse projects in which he is deeply involved, from development, television shows, politics and beauty pageants.

Warren Buffet—Authority: Buffet said, "In the business world, the rearview mirror is always clearer than the windshield." This is how Authorities see life, and it's a valuable skill. Authorities have the ability to remember the past with great clarity, reminding others of what did happen and issuing warning not to let it happen again. Buffet has shown the ability to stick to the fundamentals of capitalism, no matter what the current mood of the markets is. He is known for being frugal on himself and has lived in the city of Omaha for nearly his entire career, eschewing more glamorous locations. Buffet understood early on that money and success aren't the same things.

Music

Rock 'n' roll is a great illustrator of Market Force in action because most great rock groups have one of each style contributing their own skills to the band:

The Beatles: John Lennon was the Control who formed the image of the band. Notice Lennon was a Market Force Control, who allowed others to get the credit. Most people didn't know how much of the driving force he was behind the band until they broke up and were exposed in their solo careers. Ringo Starr was the lovable Influence, who made the band more approachable. Paul McCartney was the Power and the glue that held the band together. George Harrison was true to his Authority personality. Despite being the guitarist, he was reclusive and the least recognizable member of the band.

U2: The drummer, Larry Mullen (Influence), said that he couldn't wait to be the band's leader until they auditioned lead singers, and Bono (Control) showed up. At that moment, he realized that his dream of leading the band would never be. When visionary Controls like Bono show up, others naturally defer to them; when poor Controls show up, others chafe. The guitarist, Edge, is the Power, and the bass player, Adam Clayton, is the Authority.

Van Halen: Eddie Van Halen is the unhealthy Control, who ultimately kicked the Influence, David Lee Roth, out of the band for taking too much of the limelight. The Power, Alex Van Halen, and the Authority, Michael Anthony, did nothing to stop the breakup, opting for security and stability, rather than unity.

The Who: Pete Townsend was the creative genius behind the revolutionary band. Keith Moon was the gregarious Influence, who ultimately drank himself to death. Roger Daltrey was the Power, and John Entwistle was the incredible bass player whose fundamentals kept the band musically relative.

Led Zeppelin: Robert Plant was the lead singer who gave them their image. John Bonham was the Influence drummer, who drank himself to death, just like Keith Moon. Jimmie Page was the Power, and John Paul Jones was the bassist who drove the music.

Nearly all solo music acts who are successful over the long term are Controls. This is because Controls like Madonna, Justin Timberlake, Lady Gaga, Neil Young, Beyoncé, Eminem, and Prince understand how to brand themselves over the changing times and tastes of the market. When Influences (like Johnny Cash, Jimi Hendrix, and Elton John) or Powers (like Elvis Presley and Bruce Springsteen) become famous, it's usually through extreme talent or because they partnered with Controls who fashioned an effective image for them. When Authorities like Dave Matthews or Bob Dylan are successful long-term, it's because of their attention to detail and perseverance.

These examples show the importance of working in teams. The beginning of Market Force is to become self-aware so that you can understand your contribution to a community. However, the goal is to become community-aware so you can understand and appreciate the contributions of others.

For instance, self-awareness will help in your marriage, but true partnership begins when you understand the strengths and weaknesses your spouse brings. Then you can maximize the strengths and minimize the weaknesses of your (marriage) community. In business, self-awareness allows you to become a stronger employee; however, the group awareness that comes from understanding Market Force allows you to partner with those who help you build a stronger (business) community.

It is teams that change the world. When we credit change to a person, such as Alexander the Great, Napoleon, or George Washington, we are really recognizing someone who had the capacity to attract talent to the community and then give the space for those talented people to flourish.

10

A CLOSER LOOK AT STYLES

The next best thing to being wise oneself
is to live in a circle of those who are.

C. S. Lewis

We tend to assign what's going on with us to the people around us. Another way of putting it is that we accuse others of our own faults or virtues. This isn't a new thought; most people call it *projection*. The idea is that if someone thinks everyone else is lying, she is probably a liar. If someone is the hyper-jealous type, he's probably a cheater. What is talked about less often is that this works the other way as well. This is why innocent-minded people tend to be naïve about the ill intent of others. Someone who is extremely honest tends to be more easily deceived, because it doesn't occur to him that someone in the transaction may be lying or have bad intentions.

This has important implications in Market Force because we tend to assign our own style to others. We accuse other people of thinking the way we do and speaking from the same concerns we have. This can hurt a relationship, when we think we're meeting the other person's concerns (based on what ours would be), when in reality we're stopping the action.

Controls and Influences are naturally offensive in a transaction and Powers and Authorities are defensive. Offensive players force the action (change) and defensive players resist the action, in order to ensure structure and quality, before proceeding.

When I first became a CEO of a company that was filled with analysts, I removed many of the rules and structure around the company that seemed to be overly constrictive. As an offensive player, I loathe rules and structure, and I thought these were great moves that would increase morale. I told everyone what the vision was and gave the autonomy and tools to get us there.

As an analytical company, most of the employees were Powers and Authorities and, rather than seeing the removal of policies as freedom, they saw instability. The company stumbled. Managers from across the company lined up to insist I give them more rules. One statement I heard over and over was, "We just don't feel like we know what we're supposed to do anymore."

There are several common ways the styles accuse others of their own way of thinking. Controls respond to blunt, pithy confrontation. They want the short version of the story and prefer the person get straight to the point. There is a breakdown when they assume others are the same. When it comes to confrontation, Controls often do not fully communicate their points, assuming much of what they are saying is "obvious" and therefore they don't set a foundation for their criticism.

In trying to constructively criticize another style, especially Powers, Controls can be hurtful and offensive, because they communicate to someone else in a way they would learn best, but not how the other person would learn. Power can see the confrontation as an upsetting moment in their lives, whereas Control has forgotten all about it by the end of the day.

The opposite is true of Authority. They respond to facts. When confronting an Authority, you need to have all of your facts spelled out and remove all possible arguments. They will almost always respond to confrontation with a barrage of questions, establishing whether they have to accept your assessment, based on whether you have enough data. Consequently, they approach confrontation the same way.

They want to walk the person carefully from A to Z, hitting every letter of the alphabet along the way. They want to make it clear that they have thought this through and have all the data to back up their points. The other three styles struggle with this, but especially Control. They'll quickly adapt a "Get to the point" posture, and more often than not, they'll say it. Where Authority thinks they are making their case, because this is how they prefer to be treated, they are often alienating their audience and their assessments are lost.

The mistake I made when I took over the company I mentioned above was a classic offensive player error. Offensive players thrive in freedom and a lack of structure. They're often rebels without a cause, breaking the rules, simply for the sake of breaking the rules. They assume, therefore, that others are the same.

In fact, Power and Authority are the opposite. Power and Authority love the rules, as long as they believe the rules are there for a reason. Most people have heard stories of long-time convicts who commit a crime as soon as they're released from prison so that they can go back. They miss the stability and security that the routine of prison provides. These stories were never told about an Influence.

Powers love to be in groups. If they're assigned a new project, they immediately form teams and gather qualified people around them. They provide structure around getting that project done. They'll often name the project and have T-shirts made up for all the team members. They become suspicious of others who don't seem to want to jump into their nest, because they love to be on teams and can't imagine someone who wouldn't.

Influence will often chafe at the team that Power has established and seem to have one foot in and one foot out. They may be very productive for the team, but they just won't accept their position the way Power demands. Influence bleaches the T-shirt and writes "I just gotta be me" across the team name.

Power can see this as threatening, because they can't understand Influence's insistence on autonomy. Power will demand that Influence "toe the line" and "be a team player." In the end, Powers can throw a key Influence team member out, because they start to see them as an enemy, not understanding their need for individuality.

Think of Dennis Rodman on the 1990s Bulls. He always seemed half-committed with his earrings, smirk, and dyed hair. He never seemed to give Phil Jackson or Michael Jordan proper respect, yet he showed up with intensity for every game and was an indispensible member of the team. A lesser coach or star player would have thrown him off the team. Instead, Coach Jackson and star Jordan harnessed his energy and won championships.

The Clock

Market Force is a consequence of accelerating a transaction. When you are in your proper place in a transaction, you accelerate the momentum of the team and you gain Market Force. Brute Force is the opposite of Market Force. It occurs when the transaction is slowed or halted because people are inserting themselves where they don't belong. Their insecurities and selfishness cause the negatives of their style to disrupt the transaction and the team.

Because of this, the four basic styles actually translate into eight different possibilities of behavior. This is because each style can be Brute Force or Market Force in their contributions. Which place they are in their behavior can have a distinct impact on which traits are dominant.

A style acting in Brute Force will exhibit the dominant negative aspects of their style as well as aspects of the style counterclockwise, but in a negative way. Styles acting in Market Force will demonstrate their positive traits, as well as the traits of the style, clockwise to them in a positive way.

Brute Force Control will not only demonstrate their own negative traits but will also move backward into micro-management, obsession with details, risk-averseness, dwelling on the past and other things that are usually strengths for Authority, but are produced in a counter-productive way by Brute Force Control. Market Force Control will show up with their positive traits, but also move forward into positive Influence traits such as contentment in the present, flexibility, valor, valuing relationships, and so on.

This is true of all four styles: Brute Force Influence shows negative Control traits (dominating, know-it-all, argumentative); Market Force Influence shows positive Power traits (creating space for others, focusing on the task, leveraging relationships to form teams); Brute Force Power shows negative Influence traits (scattered, rebellious, quitting rather than persevering); while Market Force Power shows positive Authority traits (persevering, attention to detail, quality-focused); Brute Force Authority shows negative Power traits (quantity over quality, gossiping, forming gangs rather than teams), while Market Force Authority shows positive Control traits (visionary, fearless, ambitious).

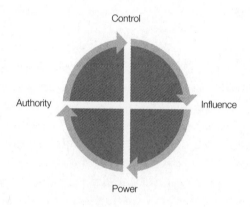

Notice the graph looks like a clock with Control at twelve o'clock, Influence at three o'clock, Power at six o'clock and Authority at nine o'clock. Some people will say, "I feel like I'm mostly a Power, but definitely have some Authority characteristics. I feel like I'm at seven o'clock, rather than six o'clock." This may be. They may be a Power who typically acts in a Market Force fashion. Many Controls (if they're honest) will say they feel like an eleven o'clock Control. They definitely exert Control traits but can become sidetracked with their past or with concerns over risk, becoming defensive in transactions, rather than offensive. They are Controls who act Brute Force a majority of the time.

People who naturally act Market Force are often harder to identify as a particular style initially because they are demonstrating good traits from both their natural style and the one ahead of theirs. People locked in Brute Force cycles are easy to identify because the negative traits of their style are so obvious and dominant.

Brute Force Control

In their need for certainty, they lose their ability to generate possibilities, and become obsessed with minor details. They make decisions rashly without understanding all of the issues and possible solutions because they're anxious to move toward certainty. They may have good ideas and insight, but will not act upon their understanding because actions may prove them wrong, which they can't tolerate. Victim Controls are usually dictatorial and abrasive, issuing orders without a reason for doing so and without consideration for the people involved. They are the types that change the radio station in the car for no other reason than to be in control of the radio.

They are overbearing and have difficulty seeing things from outside their own perspective. They usually live in an alternate universe where they are sure of things that don't exist. They cannot hear what people are saying to them because they are so locked into their own perspective. In many aspects, they think of themselves as successful and forcefully voice their opinions, even though they have accomplished nothing and have no real knowledge about the thing they are pontificating about.

Victim Controls are often guilty of "one-upmanship." They have a compelling need to tell the better story: they caught the bigger fish, or their car is faster. "You think this is cold, I'll tell you what cold is!" One can see this in talk shows. Most of the hosts are Controls, because a dream job for many Controls is one where they get to opine endlessly. One guest makes a series of points that the other guests ignore, spouting their own points as if the first person never said anything. You have two Brute Force

Controls talking at each other, not listening to a thing the other person is saying.

More introverted Controls become drawn into themselves if they resign themselves to being victims. They can fall into resignation in life and become lazy. Though they have ideas, they jump enthusiastically from idea to idea, without following through on anything, always armed with blame for who kept them from being successful. These types usually have their excuses for failure ready before they even get started.

Market Force Control

This group has the innate ability to change the world. They can be revolutionaries, dreaming of big ideas and having the ability to get others to see them and follow. They intuitively understand people and situations and know how to make wise decisions quickly. They comprehend situations well with little information, leaping ahead of others in their group in understanding the entirety of the situation. Life comes easy to Controls, because they see through the haze that others live in and see situations clearly.

Market Force Control Motto:
I like the dreams of the future better than the history of the past.
Thomas Jefferson

They draw others to them because they are aware of all the possibilities, which makes them adept at solving problems. They are filled with ideas and are able to get others enthusiastic about what they dream about. Their ability to see clearly allows them to cut through facts swiftly and make quick and accurate judgments.

They naturally take charge in situations, seeing things as they will be in the future, allowing them to make snap decisions in the present about things that confound other styles. Because they are so driven to change the world, they are almost always found in leadership, or in creative, independent careers such as surgeons or architects. They have the ability to see where an organization is headed and have the decisiveness and conviction to maximize direction or change it as need be.

Controls are typically very good debaters because of their ability to cut straight to the point of any issue. They are usually very social and attract talented people to themselves due to their quick minds and ability to help others to understand life.

Brute Force Influence

Influences can be irresponsible with a tendency toward flippantly taking risks. They may lead their community into uncomfortable financial situations, or simply disappear when things get uncomfortable. If they are stressed, they will become overindulgent and place more importance on immediate sensation and gratification than on their duties and obligations. When their world is falling apart and others need them, they're at the bar.

They are generally unaware of consequences and therefore can become overwhelmed. They can devolve into simplistic explanations for their situations and apply these explanations to practically any problem that arises. They resent any and all authority and can often go to great lengths to rebel. These are the people you find in the middle of the highway at night, daring cars to run them over. Their emotions are out of control. They are happy one moment and crying the next. These are the drunks that befriend you at the bar and then try to pick a fight with you.

Brute Force Influences will often destroy their families or organizations in a reckless need to avoid responsibility. These are the people who go out for ice cream and never return. Freedom and individuality become their gods and everything else is sacrificed for their need to avoid accountability. For this reason, Influences are prone to addiction and obsessiveness.

I had a friend who was a land developer, who had created a high-end mountain community in Colorado. He was an Influence who had collected $15 million from friends, got a loan, and spent $40 million putting together what was to be a really special development. Just before he started selling parcels, the bond market collapsed and he couldn't get the lots released to sell.

The bank foreclosed and the investors lost everything. His business partner (an Authority) walked away from him and never spoke to him again. I took my friend out to lunch and watched him drink four glasses of wine. When he ordered a fifth glass, I asked how he was doing.

He said, "What? I relax by having a glass of wine with lunch."

I asked him again how was he really doing.

"I can't remember the last time I slept, and I drink a quart of scotch a night," he said defiantly.

I just nodded and told him to call me anytime he needed a friend. Influences in such a state don't need advice; they're drowning in the present and can't see beyond it. When they're buried like that, they just need a genuine relationship.

Market Force Influence

These people are delightful to be around. They are the life of the party, and everyone wants to be their friend. They have an abundance of energy and enthusiasm, wearing the perpetual smiles of people who are in love with life. They get excited about things and have the ability to motivate others. They're always trying to bring others along for the ride. They can sell almost anything because of their likability and enthusiasm.

They are spontaneous risk-takers with an ability to improvise in any situation. They love people and enjoy being the center of attention. They relish excitement and drama in their lives. They're usually great storytellers and love to make people laugh. They are usually very empathetic and concerned for other people's feelings. They're generous and warm and are quick to volunteer to help. They are very observant of mood, and sense when others are uncomfortable or depressed. Influences are the first to sense when a meeting is going well or poorly and can react swiftly to the mood.

Market Influence Motto:
You don't learn to walk by following rules.
You learn by doing, and by falling over.
Richard Branson

Influences give the impression that nothing ever gets to them. They never seem stressed and are the ultimate at being cool under pressure. Like Joe Montana on the Super Bowl drive, they just seem not to care. When others are strained with worry, Influence just shrugs and says, "Who wants to grab a cup of coffee?" This attitude gives confidence to others and can relax the team so they can perform.

Brute Force Power

Powers don't usually express their negative feelings, keeping things inside. These can build up inside until they turn into resentment and then judgments and bitterness. In the face of criticism, they fall apart, becoming depressed, ultimately becoming obsessively pessimistic and perpetually down on themselves. They spend their time imagining all of the things that might go wrong. Their motto becomes, "I can't do anything right."

Because Brute Force Power is already perpetually down on themselves, it does no good to point out anything negative, because you are simply providing them with evidence for what they have developed the habit to see. They eventually develop the habit of sabotaging themselves and their team in their need to prove their inadequacy.

Powers can go the other direction as well, allowing their resentment of others to show up as passive-aggressiveness. They can become fixated on revenge. Powers can appear pleasant on the exterior but completely sabotage others. The cliché "stabbed in the back" was originated to describe Brute Force Power. They are cowardly and petty, constantly fighting battles with people who don't even know they are an enemy.

They need to control their environment in an obsession for structure and to stop change. They can be extremely insecure and focus all of their attention on pleasing others, while secretly stewing in resentment toward those they are pleasing. They can be helplessly oversensitive, imagining bad intentions when there weren't any and constantly on the lookout for who offended them. They are notorious for judging others because of their facial expression or the inflection in their voice, when there was nothing to be offended by. They can destroy an organization from the inside and others will never even know it was happening.

Market Force Power

These individuals love to bring people together. They are naturally kind, always seeing the best in people. They are great listeners and good at understanding different points of view. These people need to be liked and genuinely like others.

Market Force Powers are extremely dependable. They are accountable for their responsibilities and have a strong sense of duty.

They value security and see what needs to be done before anyone else does, and then they do it. If you are in a meeting and
complain it is too hot, it is a Power who will jump up to find the
thermostat to make sure everyone is comfortable.

Market Force Power Motto:
Opportunity is missed by most people because
it is dressed in overalls and looks like work.
Thomas Edison

Powers take great joy in doing a good job and in pleasing
others and don't see a need to stand up and take credit. They see
it as a pleasure to do their duty and do it well. Often behind a
larger-than-life Control who gets all the credit for success, there
is a Power who did all the work and looks for no accolades.

They invariably make people feel good about themselves.
They are sensitive to other's feelings and are always keeping
peace. Powers will persist until the job is done and never expect
others to do something they can do themselves.

Brute Force Authority

Brute Force Authorities are often frozen in fear. They see nothing
but except how things could go wrong, living their lives in visions
of doom. They can become intolerably rigid and obsessed with
details, driving people around them crazy. Brute Force Authority
thinks the solution to every problem is more rules.

Convinced they are the only one on the team with any value,
they are sure they're being taken for granted. They blame failures
on others and become arrogant. Brute Force Authorities are often insufferable liberal activists or right-wing religious zealots.

In either case, they are completely intolerant of any other viewpoint. Debating with them is exhausting, because no facts suffice. They hear only what supports their viewpoint.

Brute Force Authorities are aloof and reserved. They are incapable of giving praise or positive support and generally view other people as a pain. They will never risk being wrong and therefore cannot make a decision. They look for success and then show up claiming the credit. Most shocking to their victims is that they actually believe it.

In the Marine Corps, we would say of these people that they are first in line to eat and last in line to die. In other words, they'll push their way to the front of the chow line and to the back of the fighting line. They are quick to claim their rights and will never claim their duty.

Market Force Authority

These people are extremely faithful and loyal. They care deeply about those close to them, although they usually express their affection through actions, rather than words. They can take a task and define it, organize it, plan it, and implement it. They will persist through anything to accomplish a task they believe in. They see their success simply as the natural fulfillment of their obligations and are surprised when people praise them.

Market Force Authority Motto:
The miracle, or the power, that elevates the few
is to be found in their industry, application, and perseverance
under the promptings of a brave, determined spirit.
Mark Twain

They are always looking for a dilemma to solve, constantly looking for a way to improve their environment. They honor traditions and laws, and have clearly defined standards and beliefs. They know what has worked well in the past and possess no tolerance for people who do not value the established order. They live in a world of facts and value, competence and efficiency.

They can consolidate multiple ideas into structured patterns. They take pride in taking other people's ideas and making them better. Authorities can be innovative because they see all of the details and process them efficiently. They can summarize details in a way that the team can understand and then develop systems of efficiency around those details.

Each style has its favorite telltale statements or ways of thinking, when they are falling backward into Brute Force. If you're a Power, you may not say "Everyone is unfair" in quite that way, but that becomes a prevailing thought process, degenerating into a consistent Brute Force attitude. Listen for these thought or speech patterns in yourself or others as signs of moving Brute Force.

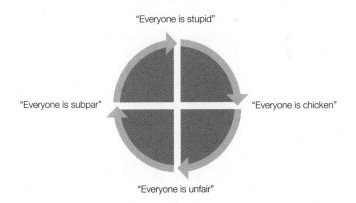

There is No Neutral

In the constant transactions of life, you are either appropriating Market Force or you are not. You are either going forward or you are falling backward . . . but you are never staying still. These are not personality descriptors. Your style is the place from which you naturally come in a transaction and the place to which you automatically go in a moment of chaos.

To analyze your personal character, ask yourself whether you more consistently occupy Market Force or Brute Force. More revealing than actions are your thoughts. Look at the descriptors of your style again. Do your private thoughts tend more toward Market Force or Brute Force? What you think is who you are before you have the chance to put on your survival face. What you think is really how you contribute to your world, whether you are aware of it or not.

Most Brute Force people are unaware of the extent to which they poison the world around them, thinking that their survival act is fooling people. Conversely, most Market Force people are unaware of what a delight they are to the world around them and how much they have improved their world without even being conscious of it.

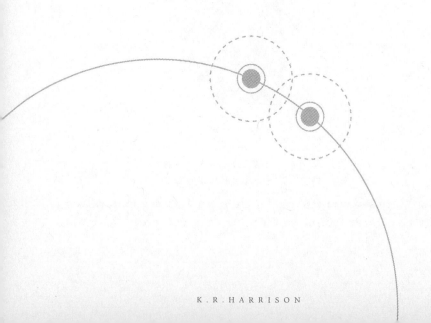

11

HIDDEN THOUGHTS AND INNER HAUNTINGS

Nothing can stop the man with the right mental attitude
from achieving his goal; nothing on earth can help the man
with the wrong mental attitude.

Thomas Jefferson

The very qualities that make each style strong are also the qualities that, if misapplied, can bring great destruction to themselves or others. Said another way, a person's greatest gifts can also be their greatest curses. Each style has hidden thoughts and inner hauntings, unique to themselves.

Since we tend to project onto others what is going on within us, we also tend to assign our own faults or thought processes to them. However, as you can see in the following, we often apply our unique shortcomings to people who think in completely different ways. It is helpful to know the things that haunt you and that others suffer the same things. It is also helpful to know the unhealthy thought patterns of the other styles so you know how to offer assurance to them in a breakdown in a way that they can hear and receive.

Control: Be Careful What You Wish For

Controls often refuse to subvert their agenda for someone else's. They can be resentful for living under someone else's vision and leadership. This can apply to any organization from work to family, a board of directors to the local PTA. Controls often work to seize leadership, even though they often have no idea how to lead or what to do once they get the position they covet. For unhealthy Control, receiving a prestigious title or the leadership position is more about not living under another's authority than in actually leading.

For Controls who resent living under someone else's agenda, the effects can be telling. They often live in secret rage, which shows up in explosion of tempers at odd times or an angry tone in a simple discussion. They often have a hostile, aggressive look in their eyes or in their tone that can be off-putting to others.

Often Controls are unaware of this. They shock themselves with their outbursts of vicious words and claim that this is not really who they are. The fact is, they are so used to living with an inner rage that they don't realize it's not a normal way for most people to exist.

Less confrontational Controls internalize their resentment. They possess the same rage but never vent it. They may become hypochondriacs. These types seem to be perpetually suffering from high blood pressure, back pain, allergies, or whatever flu or cold bug is going around. They seek incessant control over every detail of their lives, often becoming obsessive-compulsive. In their insecurity and hidden rage, they seek certainty at any cost. If they are unable to gain leadership, they turn their resentment into resignation, often becoming lazy.

If, unfortunately for the group, they do take leadership, they end up resenting both those who promoted them and those serving under them. For this group, nothing is ever their fault. They will go to their graves blaming someone for everything in their lives that didn't work out.

They are incapable of genuine apology. Their general attitude seems to be that if they were given ultimate control and it wasn't for the incompetence of all the people around them, things would be the way they should.

I once had a senior executive who was the picture of professionalism—and the perfect example of Brute Force Control. In time, his growing resentment of living under my agenda began to show itself. Though he was respectful to me, he became increasingly hostile to employees behind my back. He often enacted nonsensical policies that ended up restricting creativity and fostering an atmosphere of fear in his division.

In less than a year, he had an increasing number of trips to the doctor and emergency room. He missed work constantly with back spasms, asthma, allergies, flu, and sick children. As his division began to fail and morale fell, he blamed his employees, saying they were all "incompetent and unmotivated." He asked for permission to fire several of our top and most longstanding managers, because he couldn't "get control" with them around. He insisted that they poisoned the culture "with all their talk of autonomy." His solution? "I need to teach these people to get in line!"

When I asked about his own failure in sales and execution, he said that our clients were "stupid" and didn't know what they needed. I summed up our conversation by saying, "So, if we had all new employees and all new clients, then you could be successful? Is there any possibility that it isn't everyone else—that it's just you?"

I ended our meeting and required him to come back in a week with an answer to my question and a plan to turn his division around. When he returned, his plan was simple: If I would just give him complete control to run the firm, he could be successful. He couldn't possibly be expected to be successful when all he ran was a division. He had lost all grasp of reason and his only explanation was that he needed ultimate authority and the ability to eliminate anyone who questioned him.

Little progress can be made by merely attempting to repress what is evil. Our great hope lies in developing what is good.

Calvin Coolidge

When I fired him, morale among his staff quickly improved. He had descended into the depths of unhealthy Control, becoming a tyrant, sure the answer to his failure was more control and a heavier hand. This is a classic example of a Control in complete breakdown. They become blinded to their own failings, blaming everyone around them, leading them to fight imaginary battles that only exist in their head.

Influence: A Shortsighted View of the Future

Influence can rise to great heights of success but crash hard in failure, because they haven't prepared their emotions the way other styles have. The future just doesn't occur to them. An Influence friend of mine had a Newfoundland, a huge dog that was sixteen years old. When I asked him what he was planning to do when his dog died, he just stared at me and then started to tear up. "I've never thought about it before," he said. When I pointed out that his dog had already lived beyond its life expectancy, he just shook his head and said that he'd never thought about his dog dying.

Life often takes Influences by surprise because they simply don't worry about consequences. The very thing that allows them to be heroic and inspiring while others are frozen in fear can also drag them down. This is why so many amazing war heroes commit suicide when the fighting stops. They were Influences who hadn't prepared themselves for when the war ended.

Because they live so completely in the present without the worry so many others feel, Influences can experience great joy and contentment. However, the thing that allows contentment can also be a curse that leads many to addiction. Influences often lack self-control. In the legend of the Knights of the Round Table, King Arthur is a Control who leads the kingdom with great wisdom. He trusts Lancelot implicitly. Lancelot is an Influence who's the personification of valor. He ultimately betrays Arthur and takes his wife because he can't resist her beauty, destroying the kingdom.

Influences attract people to themselves because they tend to be full of life. Because of this, they can be self-destructive but also naturally adept at sensing mood. At their best, Influence can be extremely sensitive to people and their feelings. At their worst, they can allow the suffering they see in others to affect their own mood or use this skill to manipulate people for their own short-term satisfaction.

Influence can have myriads of friends but appear completely disloyal. This is because they can become obsessed with their need for freedom. They will often sacrifice relationships and even themselves in their need not to feel tied down. Brad Pitt's character in the movie *Legends of the Fall* is classic destructive Influence. He attracts everyone to him, but when they come to count on him, he runs away. He flees to war, then to the sea. No one can resist his charisma even though destruction goes with him. At the end of the movie, the narrator says that his character was a rock that they all broke themselves upon.

Power: Mixing Virtue with Vice

Think of all the positive qualities of Powers: they are hard workers, organizers, loyal team members, champions of truth and justice. When you consider the flip side of these virtues, you have the haunted Power. In its base form, you can see it in a clique of middle-school girls. They form their group out of insecurity, mocking, bullying, and excluding everyone not in their clique. They're terrified of saying the wrong thing or doing anything that might violate their standing in the clique.

Because Powers do not create identity, but gain it from the people with whom they associate, they live in terror of exclusion because they might lose their identity. They can watch other students reduced to tears without lifting a finger to help, lest they end up as a cast-out of the clique.

Find a clique like this, and you will nearly always see a Control who rose to the top and dictates the rules to the group. They follow her orders blindly, fearing that she will exclude them from the clique if they lose her favor.

This plays itself out as Powers get older, as the behaviors become more subtle, sophisticated and cruel. When they are unhealthy, Powers can be vicious thugs as leaders or mindless followers as team members.

Nazi Germany was a perfect example of unhealthy Power run amok. Germany is a Power society. You can see it in their work ethic, you can see it in the cars they build (all of them promise to give you an identity if you drive them). Once Hitler proved himself competent, the Powers followed him unquestioningly.

Their excuse for inhuman cruelty was that they were simply following orders. These brainwashed Powers actually believed this was a valid excuse when they made it. Not all Nazis were Powers (Hitler was an Influence), but the movement was locked in a Brute Force Power mentality. They ignored horrible atrocities around them, terrified of speaking out for fear of losing the false stability the Nazis provided.

Hitler blamed the French, the British, the Lutheran church, the Jews, and the Communists for the problems of Germany. Many Germans valiantly fought the rise of the Nazi party, but Powers were attracted to the structure and identity they imposed, especially after so many years of unrest and uncertainty. True leaders move people toward a common cause. False Leaders move people against a common enemy.

The mafia is another example of haunted Power. It is an exclusive organization that provides its members with identity and stability. To belong to the mafia is the ultimate exterior identity. It stands for Brute Force Power as a gang of thugs, ready to enforce their will on anyone who doesn't bow to their identity. The greatest danger is not to go against their greed, but to not validate their identity as thugs. The mafia values the code word of Power: respect. To disrespect them is to invalidate them.

The reason Powers often tolerate awful injustice, even though their core concern *is* justice, is because they convince themselves that change won't make a difference, so they resolve to tolerate and survive.

Authority: Secure with the Status Quo

Authority can live in mortal terror of change and progress. When faced with change, Authority resorts to a form of administrative Puritanism. The results are intolerance of opposition, unbreakable belief in their own narrow view, and disproportionate counterattack.

Left to their own devices, Authority will often struggle with maintaining focus on their own long-term intentions. This struggle is obvious as the most difficult move for each style is the next move in the market force cycle. For Authority, that move is intention/ declaration (Control). With a natural inclination toward reviewing the past and a predisposition toward preserving their security, the thought of holding to one direction is often overwhelming for Authority.

What feels natural is to focus on the past. In terms of the transaction, this means Authority is often clamoring to prove their value based upon a preceding transaction. Thus, Authority attempts to win small battles that have nothing to do with the overall war.

The trigger for this reaction is a concern for being recognized as competent by others and for making sure no one is overlooking their value. Instead of negotiating for their conditions upfront, they wait until the end of a transaction to attempt to prove to others that they were the most valuable person in the transaction. Whether they are correct about this notion is less relevant than the fact that Brute Force Authority people are often celebrated for leaving—as opposed to celebrated for their contribution.

The only way out of this recurrence for Authority is to have clarity of an intended future and to passionately negotiate for the conditions they need before implementation. While this appears more risky than the "deliver then demand" approach used naturally

by Authority, it is the only method for ensuring long-term success. Any deviation from this path causes Authority to stew with
resentment toward others in the transaction. At this point, their
focus will shift away from the big picture toward winning in the
short run.

Because Authority wakes up in the morning looking for a
dilemma, they can be very effective teammates. But this characteristic can also be a curse. Often Authority uses this trait as an
excuse to avoid choice. They lock themselves into the horns of
the dilemma and declare there is no choice. Their most effective
manner is to claim that no options meet their standards and
they are therefore unable to choose a solution. They are content
to paralyze the team.

It isn't that they can't see the solution.
It's that they can't see the problem.
G. K. Chesterton

I once supervised an excellent chief operations officer, an
Authority and an integral part of our leadership team. While we
were growing substantially, he kept his eyes constantly on the
bottom line, keeping us from growing into bankruptcy.

Problems began when he started to purposely slow down the
growth of the company. He began stalling on new hires and new
offices in classic Brute Force Authority style, pestering people
with an incessant list of questions and claiming that we couldn't
move forward because his standards had not been met.

The growth of the company, which he had been instrumental
in, began to drive him crazy. He went on an all-out offensive to
stop any and all action, imposing burdensome policies. He took it
upon himself to approve all expense reports, working exhaustive

hours to look through thousands of reports per month and rejecting hundreds of them, sending highly productive employees in search of $10 receipts. He instituted new-hire background checks and questionnaires that were impossible to complete.

I lined up coaching for him and urged him to honestly assess his behavior, but he refused. He complained that no one was meeting his standards and he was smarter than the coach I had hired for him. The speed at which he slid into complete Brute Force mode was truly amazing. He went from being a very effective COO to a paranoid roadblock within a few months.

The final straw came when he disobeyed a direct order from me. When I asked him why he had not done what I asked, he said he didn't think it was important. I didn't react or argue; I stopped the meeting, pulled his contract, mobilized HR and the legal department, and had him dismissed within the week. His last action was indicative of Authority who has reached bottom. Orders were now optional because he was too smart for everyone, including the CEO.

This story has a bright side, however. That COO called me a year later to say that being fired was the wake-up call he needed. He reflected on the coaching and the books I gave him, and it changed his life. He became a completely different person, one who was humble and insightful, and we are friends to this day. True leadership sometimes takes time to show its effectiveness.

12

WAITING YOUR TURN

Four-fifths of all our troubles would disappear if
we would only sit down and keep still.

Calvin Coolidge

Aaron Rodgers is one of the best players in the NFL, but he's on the field less than half the game. As the Green Bay Packers' quarterback, Rodgers doesn't play defense or special teams. Despite his talent, he has to wait his turn to get on the field. If Rodgers decided that since he's a top player in the NFL, he should also play linebacker so he could use his skills as much as possible, he would be a huge detriment to his team.

The idea is absurd, but no more so than people who refuse to hand off when the cycle calls for skills other than those they have. In business or in life, people believe they have to be skilled at everything, thinking they need to be "well-rounded." That thinking creates people who attempt to be, as the cliché goes, a mile wide and an inch deep. It creates anxiety in people who are constantly compelled to work outside of their position.

Have you ever noticed that a four-bladed helicopter always takes off to the right, not straight up? It's because when an outside force is applied to a rotating body, the result of the outside force will occur approximately 90 degrees later in the plane of rotation. Since the blades swing clockwise, a helicopter takes off at a right angle to the direction it actually intends to go.

This is called *gyroscopic precession* and the same phenomenon occurs in Market Force. Notice a typical business transaction: Control exerts energy in marketing, which causes breakdown where Influence dwells in sales. As Influence exerts energy in sales, it causes breakdown for Power in production. As Power exerts energy in production, there is a breakdown for Authority at administration.

You can apply this to any practical situation. A company starts a new business line and markets it heavily (Control). The marketing creates curiosity, then demand. Sales people build on the momentum created by the demand and execute contracts (Influence). The contracts must be satisfied with work, producing the product (Power). Delivery of the product creates a need for administration, accounting, and quality assurance (Authority).

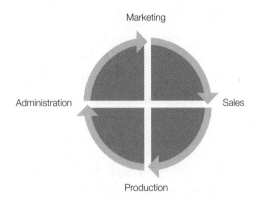

Each point on the wheel is necessary and favors one of the styles. At each point in the cycle, the styles must hand off to the next so the process can move forward. As the process moves through Authority, it must be renewed and expanded—back to Control. Market Force is the effective clockwise hand-off from one style to the next: Control (offer, intention, image) to Influence (promise, time, relationship) to Power (request, work, value) to Authority (assertion, money, choice), back to Control (back to flexibility).

A start-up company in the Silicon Valley in the 1980s is a good example. Control shows up with vision and ideas and creates companies that immediately attract Influence (think Apple and Microsoft, both founded by visionary Controls). People come to work in shorts and flip-flops and keep their surfboards and their golf clubs in their offices.

The company is completely offense-oriented. Influences see freedom and creativity and show up in droves. Momentum is formed and contracts are sold, creating huge demand for work, attracting Powers from all over the country.

Powers come to work on time wearing slacks and oxford shirts and resent the pizza parties and golf outings that the Influences love. Power feels that these get in the way of production. They ask irritating questions like, "Why do we do things this way?" They wonder about the expenditures of the company and the apparent flippancy of the Influences over receivables and delivery. The Influences chafe at the Powers, who they feel threaten their culture. Influence is tempted to pull the cycle back to their domain, where things are fun and they don't have to listen to the Powers whine about deadlines and processes.

These companies were notorious for long waiting lists, inefficiency and inability to deliver, yet demand was as high as ever. Enter Authority. The company, especially the Powers, breathe a sigh of relief as the Authorities create efficiencies, methods for getting bills paid, HR policies, proper accounting, and organizational charts.

Very quickly, however, the Powers come to resent the Authorities. They view the Authorities as impediments toward getting work done and try to stop the cycle in their domain. The company needs production and the Authority's rules, audits, and processes slow the work down.

Typically, the Authorities go too far in their love of structure and begin to stifle the organization. They begin to choke the lifeblood from the process. They insist on a dress code and more titles and hierarchy. Authorities fall in love with the feeling they had when they first appeared and the improvements they made to the company through structure.

They attempt to recapture it through more structure and more rules. They begin to see their primary responsibility as stopping all innovation, because innovation creates uncertainty and risk. Their key phrases become, "Has this been run through legal?" and "What does the policy manual say?" In fact, Authority begins to hide behind incessant and endless questioning because this grinds the process to a halt.

The cycle has completed. A company was started on an idea and someone's ability to market it, attracting those who could sell it, those who could produce it, and those who could maximize efficiency. The cycle must now be restarted and the organization is at a crossroads. It faces choice. If it goes Brute Force, Authority will refuse to release control of the process.

The right thing to do never requires any subterfuge, it is always simple and direct.

Calvin Coolidge

In their quest to stop the action, Authorities become increasingly offended by the Influences that still remain and they take it as their personal mission to hunt them to extinction. The offensive players begin to wonder why they work there.

The Influences flee to freedom from the rules and the Controls rebel at the lack of innovation (code for lack of affirmation of their ideas) and move on. The company is left with a great majority of defensive players. Powers live in resentment and anger, fighting for their stability and Authorities hold an iron grip on the company because they believe they are the only reason it exists.

Or the company goes Market Force. This is a difficult renewal because the most difficult hand off in the cycle is from Authority back to Control. Control will renew with innovation, vision, and ideas, and will have little to no data to back up their assertions. Authority is offended at Control's declarations of the future without proof, in large part because this includes risk and uncertainty, the two things Authority fears the most. Wise Authorities ask the right questions, watch the bottom line and move out of the way so the cycle can renew, waiting, as the other styles did, for the chaos of growth to swing the cycle back to them again.

The Lessons of History

One can also see this process in history. At one time, workers' rights laws were innovative and wonderful protections for the common worker. The innovation of the Industrial Revolution led to great momentum in American society, leading to an explosion of work and growth. This, however, led to a need for fairness and worker protection. The laws originally enacted to protect workers' rights for conditions generations ago have become so onerous now that business innovation has become limited.

Now, the same Brute Force Authorities who have taken over government, compiling law after law, are asking why companies are leaving the U.S. They lament the gridlock of Congress, complaining they can't pass more laws. In reality, we don't need more laws, we need less, to clear the way for new ideas. Polls have reiterated the public's growing mood of "Throw the bums out!"

In reality, this is exactly what we need. We need offensive players in government to displace the entrenched defensive players, whose time in the cycle passed long ago. They refuse to pass the torch, and the effects are obvious. America needs renewal and innovation and our entrenched leaders are doing everything they can to stop it from happening.

The Ways of the Workaholic

A failure to wait for the right time in the process is evidence of team dysfunction, and one symptom of this flaw is unhealthy work ethics in members of the community. Different styles can appear the same in their actions, but their motivations are very different—this is extremely important to understand. In order to lead, coach, or simply have a healthy relationship, it is important to know a person's style so you know why they do what they do.

Take a workaholic, for example. All four styles can become obsessed with work. On the outside they look the same:

They work long hours and when they aren't working, they're checking their iPhone. Their conversation always seems to be centered on their job, and they have little interest or time for anything else.

We tend to assign a blanket accusation of selfishness to such people and implore them to stop working so much. But notice, Controls are often workaholics, but it is not about work, it's about the Idea. If you understand the Idea, you'll understand what drives a particular Control to work so hard. If it is a broad idea of being successful, or reaching some status point, imploring Control to work less will have no other effect than causing resentment. Often Controls aren't aware of why they work so hard and have usually never voiced the reason, even to themselves.

They have some vague understanding of what drives them but have often never considered it. In this case, get Control to voice the cause for their unhealthy work habits—in essence, help them identify the Idea, then set milestones toward that goal. Celebrate each one and Control will relax after making the goal. Control wants to be acknowledged for success. Understand what their idea is, and you can understand the solution to Control's work habits.

Influence never works hard for the sake of work. Most often, workaholic Influences are locked in competition, either with someone else, or with themselves. Influences often tend to be hyper-competitive, especially in sales or production roles where results are made public.

Influence can become obsessed with winning, even if there is nothing to win. To help Influence in this situation, create a different competition. Help this person to declare victory and direct their attention to something more productive.

Power is the one style that is a workaholic by nature. They can't help it. They get their value from accomplishing. When a Power is complaining about how much work they have, they're actually bragging. They literally need to be told simply to work less.

Helping them in this situation, though, is in letting them relax in their own way. On a day off, when they are rearranging the garage and pruning the bushes, let them. It's how they relax. If you force them to relax in your way, by reading a book or taking a nap, they become resentful. Give them a list of things to accomplish and praise them for finishing. Tell them they've earned their time off and then they'll gladly relax in your way, but they need to feel they worked for it.

Authority become workaholics when they're fixated on making an impact. They can get this way in leadership positions because they don't believe anyone else is competent. So they run around behind their people redoing their jobs, or they refuse to hand off assignments in the first place.

Authorities like this will constantly complain that no one does their job right and they "have to do everything." To help Authority in this situation, ask for a detailed list of their standards of quality for a given project and then tell them to go away while you complete the list. They'll still complain but with far less gusto.

In each instance, the outside behavior is exactly the same: people who work too much. Notice, though, that the reasons are different. This is true of any behavior. Understanding a person's style is the key to understanding his core motivation and then directing behavior in a way that is most beneficial to the team.

13

INTERDEPENDENT COMMUNITIES

People who work together will win, whether it be against complex football defenses, or the problems of modern society.

Vince Lombardi

Teams are living things, and the greater the commitment from the individuals to the team, the stronger the team is. I was invited to a symposium of executives to discuss the ramifications of the financial sector meltdown in 2008. A well-known speaker was there to emcee the discussion. There were about thirty people who ran financial companies, all sitting around a large conference table. The speaker asked us to define a "successful partnership" based on the first thing that entered our minds. I was the first one to go and said, "Sacrificing one's self-interests to accomplish the goals of the team."

Everyone else shared their response, and when they finished, the moderator turned to me and said, "Your definition is awful."

He smiled to show he meant no offense and said, "I know where you were going with your definition, but your background is the Marines Corps and police. When you use words like *honor* and *character* and especially *sacrifice*, you lose people. They have no perspective to understand what you mean. They don't come to work to sacrifice—they come to make money. Period."

He was right. What I was trying to describe was an interdependent community, and they don't work based on sacrifice, unless that sacrifice is voluntary and equal among all members of the team. In other words, they work based on reciprocal contribution.

In the old world, if I was a blacksmith and you were a baker, I would give you four horseshoes for a dozen loaves of bread. Giving you the horseshoes is not a sacrifice; it is an offer based on your return offer for bread. In today's world, my offer to the team or community must be authentic, and I must also know my terms of reciprocal contribution (what I get for doing so).

You can see the need to know your style in order to understand what you bring to the team. If you are Influence, you bring the ability to create relationships, but you likely need someone else to pay attention to the details (Authority). If you are Control, you bring bold ideas and vision for the future, but you need Power to execute them.

Market Force styles team up as two different groups, and it is important to know the distinction because these are the foundations for the styles. The first is offense (Control and Influence) vs. defense (Power and Authority). The second is thinkers (Authority and Control) vs. doers (Influence and Power). Therefore . . .

Control: Thinking offensive player
Influence: Doing offensive player
Power: Doing defensive player
Authority: Thinking defensive player

The reality of these distinctions and teams are important to know because they affect how people learn, instigate, react, and perceive.

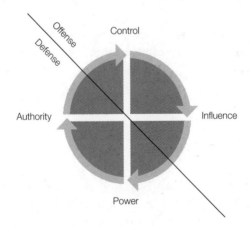

Offense

Control and Influence play offense. They initiate transactions and provide momentum. They enjoy and often feel compelled to initiate change. Offensive players keep the process moving and renewing. They avoid stagnation. Offensive players create chaos in the process, moving the transaction forward to defense, which adds structure and administration. At their best, they keep organizations moving forward and force growth. At their worst, they can mistake change for progress and gamble rather than pushing through calculated risk.

Offensive players are "homicidal." They will sacrifice people and relationships to move transactions forward. Control will sacrifice for the Idea and Influence will sacrifice for freedom and momentum, but both tend to attack others when their offense is threatened. Both can be perceived as heartless and selfish in these situations, but this is not necessarily true. When they are behaving Market Force, they are excellent at wading through people's excuses if they see the process being slowed.

Offensive players, when they are acting Market Force, will not tolerate obstacles and will move aggressively to eliminate them, even if it means hurting or eliminating relationships. Brute Force offensive players can become tyrants, eliminating those who are trying to add structure and quality to their transaction, because they see only their own point of view.

Defense

Power and Authority play defense. They naturally slow the process to add structure and administration to the chaos brought by the offense. They bring sober analysis and thoughtful deliberation, vetting the ideas and analyzing the push for change brought by offense. Defense assesses the costs and risk/reward of ideas. At their best, they keep offense on track and are reminders of the vision and mission. They ask probing questions and force offense to be deliberate and to follow through. At their worst, they can stop action, simply to alleviate their concerns for stability and security, stumping progress and inhibiting growth.

Defensive players turn "suicidal." They tend to take all of the responsibility on their own shoulders, often obsessing when they fail. Defensive players can become obsessed with their own contribution or lack thereof. They can be very loyal, sacrificing themselves for a cause they believe in. They will follow a leader who has earned their trust, throwing themselves into a project relentlessly.

They demand acknowledgment for their contributions (Power through being included or promoted to a special group, Authority through being listened to and having their assessments affirmed). In failure, though, they can internalize their disappointment. As Victims, they will become hypercritical and subvert or betray the group.

Thinkers vs. Doers

Authority and Control are thinkers—they need to fully contemplate things before they move. At their best, they fully assess the risk and the consequences of their ideas before they turn into action. They carefully plan and design their moves before allowing them to come to fruition.

At their worst, they can be frozen in inaction, obsessing on the possibility of risk and demanding certainty before taking action. They think they are researching, but they are really gathering evidence to support their inaction.

Influence and Power are doers—they often act before they fully think things through. At their best, they move ideas forward by giving them momentum. When thinkers let go of their desire to reduce risk and their demand for certainty, and move the transaction to the doers, ideas become action. Momentum is gained and production can begin.

At their worst, they move before they think, becoming impulsive and not fully considering the consequences of their actions. Doers can be impatient, forcing action and not waiting for the transaction to come to them.

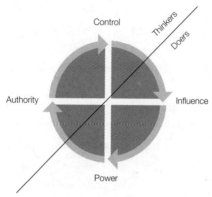

The Way of Learning

To learn is to risk revealing your incompetence. Learning exposes new distinctions that allow for more effective action. One of the strongest signals that there is something to learn is the feeling of potential humiliation—the threatened loss of one's current identity. Each style learns differently. Control learns by thinking, Influence learns by talking, Power learns by listening and Authority learns by reading.

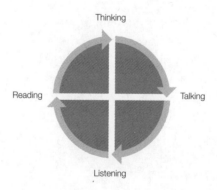

Controls are usually the slowest learners. This is for a myriad of reasons, not the least of which is that they're poor listeners. Control is often anxious to "get to the point," so they miss some of the steps along the way. Also, Control resists revealing what they don't know. In a voluntary self-improvement class, like martial arts or painting, Control will seek private lessons so they'll know more than others in the class.

Controls need time to think and process what they've learned and they can become impatient when people interrupt this process. Controls can often be heard abruptly saying, "Quiet, I'm thinking!" What they mean is that they're processing something they've learned. Controls can end up mastering something that they value if they believe it benefits their image. In learning, Controls can often be either dismissive or obsessive, depending on their initial assessment of the value of the subject and the competence of the teacher.

Influence usually learns before everyone else. This is primarily for the same reasons Control learns more slowly: Influence doesn't care about revealing what they don't know. They'll try anything and won't hesitate at the potential for humiliation. Because Influence just doesn't care about tomorrow, they can throw themselves into learning with their entire self.

Where Control is silent about their learning until they have processed enough to conceal the potential that they might not know, Influence talks excitedly about new things they're learning and wants to tell everyone else around them. The shortcoming for Influence is that once the excitement of initial learning has waned, they can become distracted and not learn completely.

Powers learn best by listening, rather than by reading. Power learns a task best by being shown its practical application. Once the task is learned, and its practical importance is understood, Power will faithfully and tirelessly carry the task through to completion. Power also learns quickly but usually learns more completely than Influence. This is because they are listeners. Power will listen intently to a subject.

The danger for Power is that they can sometimes listen for the action required and then disregard the rest of the lesson. They are people of action, anxious to listen but often only up to the point where they have a perceived action to perform. Another problem is that Power sometimes listens to get the right answer, rather than to understand the subject. Powers can be those students who get straight As on tests but completely forget the class when the semester is over. Powers sometimes have to learn the same lessons repeatedly.

Authority learns by reading. They want to have all the source information to study, and listen with skepticism until the speaker proves his mastery of an issue. Authority does not simply accept a teacher's assertions; they want to study the issue for themselves and draw their own conclusions. Authorities are thinkers and demand proof.

In a lecture, it's Authority raising her hand with questions. If the teacher answers with certainty, the questions usually fall off quickly. If the speaker makes a misstep or shows hesitancy, other Authorities' hands shoot up and the questions get aggressive. Authority can learn very completely when they accept the assertions of the teacher, and become dismissive when they don't.

14

COMMON QUESTIONS AND MISUNDERSTANDINGS

If truth is relative, to what is it relative?

G.K. Chesterton

Styles define where we come from and where we tend to revert in a moment of crisis. The more emotionally mature people are, the more they demonstrate the positives of their style and the less they demonstrate the negatives. Very healthy people are less obvious in their style, exhibiting the good traits of all styles and rarely exhibiting the negative traits of their own style. However, in crisis, both someone's character and the style from which they originate become clear.

Most people identify with their style immediately. They hear it and smile at their strengths and grin sheepishly at their weaknesses. Most are relieved to realize that they aren't alone in their habits. I knew one Control whose reaction was complete relief when he learned Market Force.

He was a good CEO but beat himself up because he changed his mind a lot. He was passionate about one direction on Monday and equally passionate about another on Friday. When he realized that it is typical of Control to change their minds when new information presents itself, he was able to grow, knowing that many leaders have this trait. He realized it was a weakness to be worked on, not a character flaw to wallow in remorse about.

Authorities are freed from guilt when they realize that one of their style traits is to resist new relationships. Powers feel liberated to know that they love to work and don't need to apologize for it. Influences realize that they're not flaky; they just love their freedom and love people.

"I Don't Know Which Style I Am!"

Most people know immediately which style they are. If one didn't immediately jump out at you, you might be an Authority. This is because Authorities have trouble making decisions and often live in fear of being wrong, so they are slow to commit. If you are Authority, you may have enacted the protective mechanism that you unconsciously have fallen back on your whole life.

You're thinking that you just need to contemplate the material presented in this book before you decide. You're dying to ask a long series of questions. What you're really saying is (1) "I need to process the data more thoroughly;" and (2) "I am still assessing whether this book has enough credibility to be believed." Go back and read the description of Authority with an open mind and your style may be clearer.

As usual, this isn't always the case. A close friend of mine, who is a poster child for Influence, also couldn't decide what his style was, even though it was clear to everyone else. I never label anyone, since they need to see their style for themselves, so that they own their self-assessment and don't feel it has been imposed on them. By asking my friend several questions, we were able to see that his reservation was that he didn't like being "put in a box."

"I'm an individual," he said. "No one can tell me who I am and how I'm going to act!"

We laugh now as he realizes his initial reaction was typical Influence. He ran toward freedom and individuality. Once he understood this is only a place he naturally comes from and serves as a default in a crisis—but that it in no way defines who he is—he was able to see himself clearly.

One of the managing directors I supervised called me one day, distraught that people were accusing him of being Control. He was offended. But he *was* a Control, and I had a hard time not laughing. When I had asked him years earlier what his goals were, he immediately answered, "To dominate the world!"

This is about as classic a Control response as there could be. I asked him what style he thought he was, and he insisted he was Influence. When I asked why, he wasn't sure. It really came down to the fact that he wanted to be an Influence. He was a devout Christian, and he found the negative traits of Control to be repulsive.

On the other hand, the positive traits of Influence (focused on others, sincere, living in the moment) appealed to him. I had to get him to see that the positive traits of Control are beautiful and the negative traits of Influence are equally as ugly as they are for any other style. The important thing is to be honest about who you are so you can embrace your natural strengths and be conscious of your natural flaws. Once he truly understood that he was a Control, his growth and maturity took off. One year later, he went from a pretty good employee to a top 10 percent performer in the company.

Your Place in the Boat

A couple of examples might make your style a bit clearer, as well as the styles of those around you. Picture a group of people in a boat in the middle of a large lake. The boat starts to sink and people panic. What do they do?

A team reacting in a Market Force way solves the problem. Control sees the problem as it is. They see the big picture and begin to shout orders, creating teams and giving them assignments. One group is assigned to fix the hole. One is assigned to help anyone who is hurt. Another is assigned to signal for help.

The Influences move forward without fear, rescuing the drowning, diving below the water's surface to locate the leak, leaping forward to help the wounded. They are unaware of the bigger picture and unconcerned with whether anyone else is doing their job; they do the job in front of them with complete abandon.

Powers look to Control for instructions. They respond to Control's confidence and assertiveness, and move forward to work hard at their task. Powers, too, are unaware of the big picture. They have a job and they are going to do it. They naturally break into teams for maximum efficiency and work together as one unit.

The Authorities join the Powers but keep their eyes on progress, looking for efficiencies. They locate better bailing instruments so the Powers can work faster, they organize lifejackets in case the boat sinks, and they throw lines out to the Influence who has rescued someone but can't get back to the boat. The Authorities are the ones who report to Control when the boat is saved or when it needs to be abandoned, providing assessments of what needs to happen next.

A Brute Force group in the same scenario reacts differently. Instead of forming teams, they break into gangs, focused on self-preservation instead of contribution. Control shouts orders but fails to see the whole picture because they are obsessed with intervening in people's failures.

They bicker with each other about who is in charge and curse those who are failing to adequately follow their orders. Influences swim for shore and hope someone will rescue them. They would rather die trying to save themselves than sit on a sinking boat, listening to Controls scream.

The Powers have no confidence in the leadership. Some attempt a coup, the thugs asserting their rights and throwing the Controls off the boat. Others whisper to their friends, forming a clique that tries to sneak the lifeboats off the back (sacrificing the larger group for their smaller group).

Authority sits in the corner, either in denial that the boat is sinking, or assessing blame and telling anyone that will hear that they had been warning everyone the boat would sink for a long time. Authority does nothing to help; they wait for the inevitable and hope people will remember they were martyrs.

How would you react? Would you be Market Force or Brute Force? In a crisis, would you naturally look to contribute, and save the group, or would you descend into self-preservation, thinking only of yourself? This is the exposure of your character, or lack thereof, and the way in which it's exposed reveals your style.

The Little Room

Imagine a tiny room with nothing in it but a table and a half glass of beer. Grab four people, one of each style, and ask them to describe what they see:

Control will look in the room for less than ten seconds and report, "It's a table and a glass half full of beer. Any idiot can see that!"

Authority will be in the room for an hour and then come out with a long list of questions and an explanation about how he can't be expected to give an answer because the instructions just aren't specific enough. When you get him more data, he can answer your question.

Power will be in the room for five minutes and report anxiously, "It's a table and a half empty glass of beer. Did I pass?"

Influence will drink the beer and forget the question.

Are the Styles Equally Divided?

No. Control is the smallest group. Also, Controls have the hardest time being Market Force. Because of their ability to see the big picture and envision the future, coupled with a need for certainty, most Controls are Brute Force. They see and they know, but they're too scared to move forward into uncertainty, living in resentment as others become successful at possibilities that Control saw far earlier but were too hesitant to move on.

Brute Force Controls who are in leadership tend to surround themselves with Authorities who will concentrate on the potential risks and provide them with the evidence for why they shouldn't move forward. Bars are filled with Brute Force Controls telling stories about what they would have done if they'd only had the chance. For them the cliché is true: "The older I get, the better I was."

Influence also seems to be a smaller segment of the population. My observation is that this is cyclical. There are fewer offensive players in society today because we have been locked into a Brute Force Authority cycle for too long in the Western world.

There is a general defensiveness in the population as we both yearn for people of vision but at the same time suspect them and stop them from moving forward. I believe this is why we're stuck in a culture of over-regulation in the United States. We demand freedom for innovation, but then support politicians who enact regulations that will keep it from happening.

Can Someone be Different Styles at Different Times?

No, but you can act in ways consistent with another style when it is needed. A common misconception is people saying that they're in "Power" mode when they're working quite a bit, or they're in "Control" mode when they're leading. Anyone can demonstrate portions of other styles when they are needed, but this doesn't make them that style.

An Influence who is starting a business may work countless hours, but this doesn't make her a Power. An Authority who just started college may go to a lot of parties, but this doesn't make him an Influence. It is a time of life during which necessity or change has caused a temporary shift from his position. They will always return to their style when things stabilize or if a crisis or breakdown occurs.

Can Someone be a Mixture of Two or More Styles?

You may see *most* of the qualities of a particular style in yourself—and sure you don't see some of the qualities. Remembering that these are core characteristics but not necessarily parts of your personality, you may have learned to behave differently in a certain circumstance.

When I was fourteen, I got a job cutting down trees for a rancher in rural Oregon. I'm a Control, so when he asked if I knew how to drive a tractor, I said yes because I didn't want to reveal my ignorance. The rancher promptly gave me a 1930s stick shift tractor to drive, and after an hour I had learned to work a clutch well enough to crash it into a tree. To this day, unlike most Controls, I'm the first to admit when I don't know something. I learned in a painful way to overcome that tendency. This is why the style flaws of a wise person are more difficult to detect—they've learned life's tough lessons. This is also why, in a moment of panic, traits about people that we didn't know were there will emerge.

This can be seen culturally as well. If an Influence comes from an Authority-driven culture like Japan or Switzerland, he may be ashamed of his freedom-loving ways and and try to suppress them. But this doesn't change the core concerns, simpy the outward behavior. The same is true of an Authority in an Influence-driven culture such as France.

Can a Person Change Styles?

No. As people mature and gain wisdom, they become more rounded, exemplifying the positive traits of their style often, showing the negative traits of their style rarely, and frequently showing the positive traits of other styles. However, they will always naturally come from their style. No matter how much an Influence grows, he will never naturally have the vision for the future that Control does. No matter how mature an Authority becomes, she will never prefer quantity over quality like Power naturally does.

Does a Person's Personality Give a Clue as to His/Her Style?

It can, but be careful. Yes, the man with the multicolored fake Mohawk hat on the ski slope who tries to cut into line is almost certainly Influence. The guy with the latest trendy skiwear who puts his hand into the Influence's chest and orders him back to his place in line is probably Control.

The woman with perfect skiing fundamentals, who is telling ski patrol that the Influence just broke the rules, is probably Authority. And the woman who shouts out to nobody in particular that everyone is just trying to have a good time and can't we all just get along is probably Power.

But be careful of assigning someone a style based on personality. This can be quite misleading. If someone is outgoing, many assume that he or she is an Influence. Not necessarily. Many Powers and Controls are very outgoing. Some Authorities can be outgoing as well, though less often. The important thing to note is that their style doesn't indicate whether or not they are outgoing, but why.

Control is outgoing for a specific purpose. They seek relationships for a reason. Some of my best salespeople are Controls. They will aggressively work a room at a convention, meeting countless people, but if they're making a relationship with someone with whom they realize there is no potential for sales, they'll drop it and move on. This is because they are interested in the relationship for the sake of a purpose (the idea), not for the sake of the relationship.

Powers can work that same room just as well, but they do it for inclusion and identity. They can't stand to be left alone and will work hard to find a group to be a part of. That group ultimately may or may not be profitable, but if it's comfortable, they'll stay.

Influence, on the other hand, is social simply to be social. They have no agenda or purpose, other than forming relationships for the sake of the relationship. Also important to note, Influence doesn't feel compelled to make relationships unless they want to. If they do not like the mood of the room or they don't "feel like it," they may simply stand in the corner. Influences can be loners if the mood strikes them.

The point is to be careful about assigning styles based solely on personality. It is the most common mistake made by people who are new to Market Force. Personalities are a good clue, but never the final clue. For instance, if someone takes control of a meeting and does all the talking, she may be a Control. However, Authorities can sometimes do the same thing. Their style is found in the cause, not the effect. Control seizes the meeting because she has an agenda and wants to drive it forward. Authority seizes the meeting because he wants to ensure people see how competent he is.

Understanding this is important in how you react. To pull the meeting back from Control, let her state her agenda, reassure her that it will be covered, and state that it is important that everyone have a chance to contribute equally. When you do this, all of the Powers will breathe a sigh of relief because they were likely building up resentment but did not want to risk direct confrontation. Now they have the space to contribute.

To pull the meeting back from Authority, do not argue with his assertions. Allow him to finish, acknowledge his contribution and assign a specific agenda to the meeting that gives others speaking slots. Notice the difference: if you acknowledge the Control's contribution and assign an agenda, she will continue to run over everyone because this is not her goal. Conversely, if you ask the dominating Authority to state his agenda, you actually give him permission to take up more space and make assessments about why he can't state his agenda—because of your incompetence.

Does Style Affect Morals and Character?

A person's style is simply his or her natural starting point of action and behavior. It has nothing to do with the quality of who they are. Different styles do find certain character traits to be more natural and certain vices to be more tempting. Again, any style can suffer from any form of moral deprivation, but they are inclined toward certain failings and core virtues.

Controls are typified by wisdom. As thinkers who naturally see the big picture, Controls are usually wise. People often seek them out for advice and Controls are able to offer them the confidence of the certainty they bring to the discussion (their motto: often wrong but never uncertain). Understand, however, that Controls certainly don't corner the market on wisdom, nor does being a Control ensure one is wise. It is simply a common trait of the style.

Influences can be incredibly virtuous and courageous. Because they live so intensely in the moment, Influence is capable of some amazing feats of heroism. They will often sacrifice their life, possessions, comfort and time for people they hardly know. When you think of the stereotype of the man that would "give you the shirt off his back," you are probably thinking of an Influence. Of course, not all Influences are this way, and they aren't the only ones who are generous and sacrificial, but it comes more naturally to them.

Powers care about others and naturally seek out and form teams. They demand fairness and justice and naturally look out for the interests of others to ensure everyone is treated equally. When they have gone morally wrong, they will sacrifice the community for the sake of a smaller community, to which their inclusion is assured.

In other words, they can be incredibly destructive to the group at large in order to support their need for security within a smaller group. It is Powers who lead a small contingent in betraying their company to go somewhere else, even if the new place isn't necessarily better. They are the ones who gossip and divide people, demanding loyalty to their cause.

Authorities are naturally prudent. They find efficiency and hate waste or indulgence. Sometimes, however, they can go too far. There's an episode of *The Simpsons* where Homer puts up a sign that helps make the neighborhood safer and is celebrated. After this, he becomes obsessed with making an impact and starts putting signs all over Springfield until the community hates him. He continues trying to get that initial feeling he had of realizing he made a difference.

Since prudence comes naturally to Authority, they are less likely to become obsessed with drinking or gambling than the other styles, especially Influence. They also look for dilemmas to solve and need to make an impact. Just like the other styles, these qualities can be ugly when turned bad. Needing to make an impact, with no idea of how, causes them to set up their own rules that naturally favor their own skills.

Authorities can suffer from self-righteousness. They'll become vegetarians and camp in front of the bank, condemning any form of development, or become leaders in a religion that claims that all drinking, gambling, and sex are evil. Whether to the political right or the left, they'll find any form of fun or innovation and do anything they can to stop it.

The initial benefit in mastering Market Force is in understanding yourself better, both in growth as a person and in revealing what your offer is. However, the truly wonderful thing about Market Force is that once you understand its applicability to yourself, you'll find it useful in understanding those around you. It is only by harnessing the gifts and offerings of others that you can truly be successful at building the effective teams needed to compete in today's lightening-fast world.

FINAL THOUGHTS

When the tide goes out,
you can see who's swimming without a bathing suit.

John Cundiff

If you go to cities like Jakarta or Manila, you will see beautiful tropical landscapes marred by the scars of people. Water lilies compete for sunlight with the growing mountains of trash that float down rivers. Shacks made of plywood mark the homes of the middle class. People use the streets as their bathroom in broad daylight. Crime is rampant and life is cheap. The poor look at the shacks with envy since they live in "garbage mountains." These are heaps of trash, several stories high and many blocks long, which have formed throughout the cities, radiating their stench and disease. These mountains have tunnels and walkways, built by the ingenious poor, for their shelter and protection.

I have a group of friends who travel the world helping the unfortunate. They take their motto from the Bible: "Pure and undefiled religion before our God and Father is this: to look after widows and orphans in their distress" (James 1:27). In other words, true religion is helping those who can't help themselves. These volunteers are no ordinary people. They are a strong, interdependent group that is fully committed to one intention: helping the needy everywhere in the world.

They are special in another way as well. The group is primarily made up of achievers—Victors of the highest order. They are former military Special Forces, generals, prominent business people, scientists, and entrepreneurs. They show up at major catastrophes with food, water filtration, protection, and education. They are completely self-sufficient, and they ask for no publicity.

These men gathered the families that lived at a garbage mountain in Jakarta and asked, "What kind of industry can you run? If you can think of it, we'll help you implement it." The people came back the next day with their answer. There was no industry. They were the helpless poor, barely surviving. They didn't need education; they needed food and clothes.

"Not good enough," my friends said. "We didn't come here to give you charity. Tell us what you will do to help yourselves and then we will help you accomplish it. If you do nothing, we will do nothing." Two days later, the people returned. Faced with a dilemma, they formed teams and leaders stepped forward. They had their answer. They could recycle plastic, which was abundant in their dump.

My friends helped them to form a business plan, create an operational structure, and a process to handle money. Then they lent them $5,000 to start their group. Within one month, seventeen families were being completely supported by the new company, and they remain so several years later. People were fed, the environment benefitted, and Jakarta had a new industry that could clean up some waterways. The $5,000 was paid back within the year.

This is Market Force in action—a group of Victors with an offer to be a solution to a problem. They make their offer and wait for their turn in the cycle, standing back to let others make their choice. When the offer is accepted, they step up in the transaction and lives are dramatically improved.

Back to the Streets of South-Central Los Angeles . . . Remember my story about the man who was inciting the riot while my partner and I worked to save lives? Can you see now that he was a Control who was able to immediately attract a team? Within moments, he was surrounded by people willing to risk injury or jail, merely because he said so. Amid the chaos, he conveyed certainty to others and a team formed around him. He was a true leader, though not for a positive purpose. When confronted in a way that recognized his contribution, a constructive intention for his team was formed and lives were saved.

Katherine Hepburn said of Spencer Tracey, "For him, acting comes easy and life comes hard. For me life comes easy, but acting comes hard." Your life is a constant series of transactions, some of which will be breakdowns and crises. When you know your identity and your offer, life comes easy because you aren't wasting time and emotion on how to act or what you should do.

You are able to see things as they actually are, and react to meet them from the foundation of who you are.

John's quote at the start of this chapter refers to the fact that when chaos occurs, people are revealed for who they are. Victors are often manipulated by Victims because they simply cannot conceive of someone who wouldn't take opportunity when it is offered. When they see Victims in their failure and blame cycle, they are frequently taken in.

They believe that if people just had the chance, they could succeed. Too often, Victors offer others opportunities, watch them fail, listen to their story, and then blame themselves. Victors must learn to observe what is and seek each other out and form productive teams. They must learn to ignore the howls of the Victims who scream, "Unfair! Greedy! Heartless! What about me?"

Victors must be armed with an understanding of who they are, what the world around them is, and how they fit into it. Then they can form an offer to be a solution to the problems of their world. They can also then see the Victims who have no offer and are unconcerned about being a solution. In this way, Victors can avoid becoming a host to the parasites who populate our country in increasing numbers.

The choice is yours. Will you choose rage, resignation, or revolution? Will you choose to understand who you are so you can form an identity? Will you choose to understand those who surround you so you can form an offer? Will you wait your turn in the transactions of the day, allowing others to contribute until the time for your offer has come? The choice is yours and only you can make it—and you have only made the choice when you begin the pain of action.

I close with this letter from John Cundiff to his sons:

Hunting Market Force requires a warrior to be impeccable in his relationship to the unknown since it is only

About the Author

Ken Harrison started his career as a Los Angeles police officer in the infamous 77th Division of South-Central Los Angeles, better known as Watts or Compton. There, he received numerous commendations and awards. After leaving the LAPD in the early 1990s, Ken went into business where he took over a company with five offices and fifty employees and expanded it into twenty-eight offices with over 250 employees in less than six years.

In 2006, Ken sold his company to the second largest commercial real estate firm in the world, continuing to run the U.S. company and chairing the global operation. When the bond market collapsed in 2008, creating the biggest real estate recession in history, competing companies decreased their work forces or closed their doors. Instead, Ken's company doubled revenues and tripled profits by staying diligently focused on the concepts contained in this book. Under Ken's leadership, his company became the biggest commercial real estate valuation company in the world.

Ken has spoken on diverse areas of leadership to tens of thousands of people throughout the world. In the ghettos of Manila, Ken organized orphanages to maximize scarce resources; in Sydney, he advised the biggest banks in the world on their U.S. assets; and in Haiti, he organized church leaders in rebuilding efforts after the devastating earthquake.

on the other side of this threshold that the opportunity for greater Market Force identity becomes available. The only consistent access to this territory is through transaction. To master transaction you must learn how to "know what to do when you don't know what to do." This requires expansive attention like in rock climbing when your total focus is on no focus and the rock begins to reveal itself. In unknown transaction you, as a warrior, are the only familiar reference point and you must trust the strength of your intention as the transaction begins to take shape. Everyone can find the corners of a room, but where is the exact center?

The hunted are creatures of habit and thus are predictable. To become a hunter the only habit must be no habit so you can be present, outside the self, to observe what has always already been so. Your only position is that you are always repositioning like a surfer seeking the energy of the wave. The warrior knows that what looks like chaos to others is the only opportunity to capture greater Market Force.

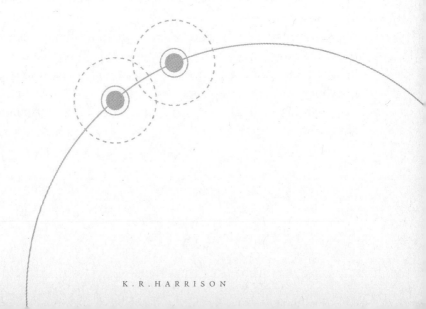